# UNIVERSAL

## An Opinionated Intro

# UNIVERSALS
## An Opinionated Introduction

### D. M. Armstrong
UNIVERSITY OF SYDNEY

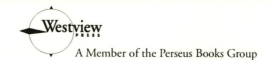

A Member of the Perseus Books Group

*Focus Series*    OCLC#
20131286

Copyright © 1989 by Westview Press, A Member of the Perseus Books Group

Published in 1989 in the United States of America by Westview Press, Inc., 5500 Central Avenue, Boulder, Colorado 80301, and in the United Kingdom by Westview Press, Inc., 13 Brunswick Centre, London WC1N 1AF, England

Library of Congress Cataloging-in-Publication Data
Armstrong, D. M. (David Malet), 1926–
  Universals: an opinionated introduction/D. M. Armstrong.
    p. cm.—(The Focus series)
  Includes bibliographical references and index.
  ISBN 0-8133-0763-5—ISBN 0-8133-0772-4 (pbk.)
  1. Universals (Philosophy). 2. Nominalism. 3. Realism.
I. Title. II. Series: Focus series (Westview Press).
B105.U5A74 1989
111'.2—dc20                                              89-34723
                                                            CIP

Printed and bound in the United States of America

   The paper used in this publication meets the requirements of the American National Standard for Permanence of Paper for Printed Library Materials Z39.48-1984.

20  19  18  17
PERSEUS
POD
ON DEMAND

For David and Steffi

# CONTENTS

# CONTENTS

This book is intended to be intelligible to the advanced undergraduate student and should also be suitable for graduate seminars. However, I hope that it will also be of interest to professional philosophers, particularly those who are sympathetic to the project of an empirical metaphysics. Since the publication of my book *Universals and Scientific Realism* in 1978, although my views have remained the same in broad outline, I have become aware of various mistakes and omissions in what I said then. The present work, therefore, besides introducing the topic, tries to push the subject further ahead.

I now think that a particular type of moderate Nominalism, moderate because it admits properties and relations, but a Nominalism because it takes the properties and relations to be particulars rather than universals, can be developed as an important and quite plausible rival to a moderate Realism about universals. In the earlier book I gave such a Nominalism only brief consideration. By contrast, in this work a battle between Nominalists and Realists over the status of properties and relations becomes one main theme.

In general, I have largely confined myself to moderate Nominalisms and moderate Realisms. That host of contemporary philosophers who unreflectively substitute classes of particulars for properties and relations I take to be immoderate Nominalists. However, many of the arguments that I bring against the more moderate Natural Class theory are also arguments against this orthodoxy. I would also classify Quine as an extreme Nominalist (although he himself would not, on the grounds that he recognizes classes and that these are "abstract" or "platonic" entities). I have criticized Quine's view elsewhere (see Armstrong 1980 and, contra,

Devitt 1980 and Quine 1980). Here I make only brief reference to his views. In the same spirit, I have given relatively little attention to immoderate or Platonic Realism about universals. Again, I do not consider, except incidentally, the view of the later Wittgenstein that the whole Nominalist/Realist controversy is some sort of a mistake, a mistake due to our misunderstanding of the workings of our own language.

For comments on a draft of this book I am very grateful to Keith Campbell, my editor Spencer Carr, Peter Forrest, Andrew Irvine, Charlie Martin, David Stove, Michael Tooley, an anonymous referee for Westview Press, and finally in very special measure, David Lewis. I thank Anthea Bankoff for the typing of the manuscript.

*D. M. Armstrong*
Sydney, Australia

# CHAPTER ONE

# The Problem

## I. Introduction

The topic of universals is a very old one. It goes back to Plato at least, perhaps to Socrates, perhaps to even earlier times. Those contemporary philosophers who pay the matter attention often speak of the Problem of Universals. So let me begin by saying what the problem is. It may turn out that it is really a pseudo-problem. That was the opinion of Wittgenstein and his followers, for instance. Quine is not far from thinking the same. But whether it is a real problem or not should not be decided in advance.

A distinction that practically all contemporary philosophers accept was drawn by the great U.S. nineteenth-century philosopher, C. S. Peirce. He originally used it in discussing semantics, but in fact it is a perfectly general distinction applicable to any subject whatever. It is the distinction between *token* and *type*. Let us follow Peirce and take a semantic example. Consider the following display:

Now we ask the question: How many words are there in this display? It is obvious that the question has two good answers: There are two words there. There is only one word there.

Peirce would have said that there were two tokens of the one type.

Once one's attention is drawn to the distinction, one can see that it applies not just to words but to almost everything. It applies to swans, electrons, patches of color, revolutions. . . . The distinction is ubiquitous. Think how it clarifies the ambiguity in the sentence 'The two ladies were wearing the same dress.'

The chief philosophical problem here is posed by sameness of type. Two different things, different particulars, can be of the same type. But 'same' seems to be a very strong word. Does it not mean *identical*? We have in our display two tokens of the same type, two instances of the same type, we can also say. If 'same' means identical here, then apparently there is something about the two 'the's that is identical. If we regard that conclusion with a philosopher's eye, the eye that tries to spot the problems that lie in the simplest things, in the most obvious things, the conclusion is rather strange. The tokens are completely separate, after all. They are in two different places. Could there really be something identical about them?

Some philosophers think that we just have to accept that the two 'the's involve something identical, something in common. After all, they argue, the word 'same' means identical, does it not? We just have to accept that the two tokens are not, after all, totally separate. Such philosophers will say that the two tokens have the same, the identical, *property*. What property? It is that rather complex and hard-to-pin-down property that makes each token a token of a 'the'.

I used to think that this line of thought had quite a bit of force, even if it was not conclusive. But I do not think this now. In order to see why the argument fails, let us look at a very interesting distinction concerning identity, a distinction that was drawn by the eighteenth-century English philosopher, Bishop Joseph Butler. Butler said that there are two senses of the word 'identity'. There is, he says, identity in the strict sense and identity in "a loose and popular sense" (see "Of

Personal Identity" in Butler 1906). The problem that Butler was concerned with was that of identity of persons and other objects over time, and although that problem does not concern us directly in this book, we do need to consider it briefly here in order to understand Butler's distinction.

We say that a certain person whom we saw today is the very same person that we saw yesterday. Does that mean that the person today and the person yesterday are actually identical? To avoid irrelevant difficulties, let us leave aside questions about minds and souls and concentrate solely on the body. "The same stone" and "the same river" would equally well do as examples.

Here is an argument for saying that a person today and a person yesterday are not strictly identical: Strict identity is governed by a principle that is called the Indiscernibility of Identicals. This says that if $a$ is strictly identical with $b$, then $a$ and $b$ have exactly the same properties. Sameness of thing gives sameness of properties. It is sometimes called Leibniz's Law. (For those who find it helpful, it can be expressed in symbols: $(\forall P)(\forall x)(\forall y)((x = y) \supset (Px \equiv Py))$, where P ranges over properties, and $x$ and $y$ range over all entities. Do not confuse this principle with the Identity of Indiscernibles, the converse of the Indiscernibility of Identicals. Identity of Indiscernibles says that if $a$ and $b$ have all their properties in common, then $a$ is identical with $b$. Sameness of properties gives sameness of thing. In symbols: $(\forall P)(\forall x)(\forall y)((Px \equiv Py) \supset (x = y))$. This second principle, which we shall meet again later on, is much more controversial than the first.)

Now consider a person yesterday and a person today. Many of the person's properties will be different on different days. The person may have been cold yesterday and may be hot today, standing up yesterday and sitting today. So it seems that we can conclude, by the Indiscernibility of Identicals, that the person yesterday is not strictly identical with "the very same person" today. The argument can be challenged, but let us go along with it here. (For myself, I think it is sound.)

3

This is where Butler's distinction can be used. We can soften the blow by saying that what we have when we speak of a person yesterday and the same person today is identity only in a "loose and popular" sense of the word 'identity'.

What is the loose and popular sense? Suppose that you are in a zoo and that you see the backside of an elephant in an enclosure. But suppose that you are behind the enclosure and another spectator is at the front and is seeing the front of the elephant. We can properly say that you two are seeing the same elephant. At the same time, though, we would agree that each of you can only see different parts of that one elephant. So in this case talk of seeing the (very) same thing only amounts to talk of seeing different parts of the very same thing. I am inclined to think that when 'the same' or 'the very same' is used in a loose and popular sense, it always involves applying 'the same' to different *parts* of the same thing, where that last phrase 'the same thing' has the sense of *strict* identity. You and the other spectator see different parts of exactly the same, strictly the same, animal.

Let us go back to the temporal case: a person (stone, river) yesterday and the same person today. I think that what we have here is two different parts of the one unified thing, the person. These parts, however, unlike the elephant case, are not spatial but *temporal* parts. In a loose and popular sense, the two parts are 'the same person'. Strictly, however, they are different temporal parts of a single four-dimensional entity, the person (the stone, the river). (But it must be noted that the doctrine that such things as persons, stones, and rivers have temporal parts as well as spatial parts is a controversial one. Philosophers who reject temporal parts for such entities have either to deny Butler's distinction between strict and loose senses of identity or else have to give a different account of the distinction from mine.)

Now, at last, we can come back to the Problem of Universals, in particular to the problem of the two 'the's. We said that although by hypothesis there are two of them, they are also in a way the same. They are instances of the very same word. It was suggested that this meant that there is something (strictly) identical about the two 'the's.

But now, with Butler's distinction before us, we can see that the argument is not so compelling as might be thought at first. Perhaps we will want to say that the two tokens have something that is strictly identical. But perhaps the identity involved is a loose and popular one. Perhaps the two tokens are said to be the same because, although strictly nonidentical, strictly different, nevertheless they are different parts of some wider unity that includes them both. Perhaps, for instance, they are both different members of the one *class*, or are both different parts of the same *resemblance structure*, or that both, although different, fall under the same *predicate* or *concept*. In that case, to apply the word 'same' to them both would be to attribute identity to them in a loose and popular sense only.

At this point I think that we can get a deeper view of the Problem of Universals. There are those philosophers who hold that when we say truly that two tokens are of the *same* type, then sameness here should be understood in terms of strict identity. The two different tokens have something strictly identical. If, for instance, two different things have the same mass, then this must be taken strictly. One and the same thing, the mass, is a constituent of the two things. Historically, these philosophers are called **Realists** and are said to believe in the reality of universals.

On the other side there are philosophers who think that when we say truly that a number of tokens are all of the same type, then all that we are saying is that the different tokens are nonoverlapping parts of some larger whole or unity (the tokens are all members of one class, or they all resemble each other in a certain way, or some other such formula). The sameness of the tokens is only loose and popular.

These philosophers hold, with John Locke, that "all things that exist are only particulars." There are no (strict) identities reaching across different tokens; there are no universals.

5

Philosophers who take such a view are traditionally called Nominalists. The word is a bit misleading. It suggests a project of explaining the unity of the tokens falling under a certain type by some linguistic device. Two things are of the same type because the same *word* (predicate) is applied to them. (*Nomen* is the Latin word for name.) That *is* one form of anti-Realism about universals, but it is far from being the only form. However, I think that we are stuck with the usage. So I will refer to all anti-Realists about universals, all those who think that identity of type is a loose and popular identity, as Nominalists.

This, then, is the traditional battle: Realists (of many different, disagreeing sorts) versus Nominalists (of many different, disagreeing sorts). The battle has been going on a long time. Antisthenes said to Plato: "I can see the horse, Plato, but not horseness." "I can see the individual object, but I can't see the universal." In the Middle Ages the battle became so heated that, so Erasmus alleged, it actually led to violence on occasions: "They wrangle with one another till they are pale, till they take to abuse and spitting, and sometimes even to fisticuffs." The fight is still going on, but I do not know when it last led to fisticuffs.

The dispute may seem a very rarefied and abstract one. And in a sense it is. But as I hope will emerge as we go on, the argument leads one into the heart of the question, What are the most general features of reality? It was a profound instinct that led Plato to put a theory of universals at the center of his metaphysics.

Before leaving the distinction between token and type, a word about identity of type. Type identity exhibits an important relativity. Consider a new display:

```
┌─────────────────────────────────────┐
│                                      │
│  THE                           A     │
│                                      │
└─────────────────────────────────────┘
```

Are the two tokens of the same type? They are not the same word. But if you take as your type just being a word, then they are of the same type. If you take as your type grammatical article, then they are again of the same type (the first is the definite, the second the indefinite, article). And there are many other types, of a more general sort, relative to which they are tokens of the same type. This relativity of identity of types is the foundation for the notion of a *property*. The two tokens each have a number of properties. The two tokens have a number of properties in common but differ in many others.

The Realist about universals will take these properties seriously (or will at least take certain selected properties seriously). The Realist will say that these properties are really there in the world, as constituents of things, and will take their sameness, where two different things have the same property, to be a matter of strict identity. Two different things have the same constituent: horseness or whatever.

The Nominalist will allow talk about properties. Such talk is impossible to avoid in practice. The Nominalist may even allow that there really are such entities as properties. But if he does admit properties, he will insist that they are not universals, that they cannot be strictly identical *across* tokens. They are particulars, as particular as the things that have them. Alternatively, he may try to explain away talk of properties in terms of some form of unity possessed by the tokens of a certain type. In either case the identity across tokens will be no more than a loose and popular sort of identity.

One reason that many philosophers have had for preferring Nominalist to Realist theories is that Nominalism, by getting rid of types, appears to yield a more economical theory. Something will be said about the attractions of economy at the end of this chapter.

## II. Class Nominalism

Having finished my introduction, I shall begin by discussing an extreme form of Nominalism. It is so extreme that I do not think that it can be satisfactory. And, indeed, my main efforts in this book will be devoted to examining more moderate forms of Nominalism, set up against a moderate Realism. But seeing some of the things that are wrong with this extreme form of Nominalism will be very useful in showing us what a plausible Nominalism would look like. I will also try to show that implausible as it is, this extreme Nominalism is more satisfactory than its main rival, another extreme Nominalism.

We have already met the view that I will examine in this section. I call it **Class Nominalism**. It is the view that for a thing to be of a certain type is nothing more than for it to be a member of a certain class. (The alternative, to be looked at in a moment, is Predicate Nominalism.)

Some things are electrons; most things are not. What is it for something to be an electron, to be of the *type* electron? According to Class Nominalism, for $a$ to be an electron is nothing more than for it to be a member of the class of electrons. The formal theory of classes, set theory, has been developed spectacularly in the last hundred years. The idea that we can give an account in set-theoretical terms of what it is to be a certain type is attractive to logicians and the mathematically inclined.

(The mention of set theory might raise a terminological question in the minds of some. Nowadays mathematicians and logicians distinguish between sets and classes. All sets are classes, but not all classes are sets. The classes that are not sets behave in a special, disorderly, way. However, the classes that we will be concerned with are quite properly behaved. So why do I not speak of Set Nominalism?

The answer is simple enough. The work done on the Problem of Universals to which I shall be referring largely antedates the introduction of the class/set distinction and uses the word 'class'. It has therefore seemed convenient to continue to use the older word.)

Instead of the word 'type' we can of course substitute more ordinary words, such as 'kind' and 'sort'. We can also speak of the property of being an electron. The word 'property' however does not sound quite natural in this case. The reason is that electrons are *substances*. (Or let us think of them as such here. Perhaps the physicists will correct us.) Natural examples of properties are colors (which electrons do not have) or mass and electric charge (which they do have). You can manufacture a property word—'electronhood'—but it does not completely convince. Compare 'horseness'. Aristotle, we may note, would have called being a horse and being an electron secondary substances. Primary substances are the individual horses or electrons.

There is a big metaphysical question here, the question of how substance types stand in relation to properties. Is being an electron analyzable in terms of properties? Is it, for instance, a conjunction of properties necessary and sufficient to make a thing an electron? Here, however, I lack the space (and inspiration) to follow the whole question up. It is my impression, for what it is worth, that contemporary science favors an account of substance types in terms of properties. In what follows, at any rate, I will concentrate on properties.

But let us go back to the main question. The idea is that the 'property' of being an electron is constituted by being a member of the class of electrons. Notice that the class of electrons is potentially an infinite one. There may be factual limits to the number of electrons, but there are no logical limits. This is sometimes put by saying that the class is an *open* class. Notice, also, that being an electron is not tied to any particular particular. The contrast is with a property like being an Australian, which is logically tied to a certain particular, the continent of Australia. Being an electron may be said to be a *pure* type, being an Australian an *impure* type. The types that

9

are of special importance for the theory of universals generate an open class and are pure. Being particular-free, in the sense of not being tied to any particular particular, they pose the sharpest problems for Nominalists.

The class of electrons has a further characteristic that suits the Class Nominalist very well. Because the class is the class of *all* the electrons, it is not a repeatable. There can only be *one* class of all the electrons. Although the members of the class are scattered both in space and in time, and the number of the members may be infinite, the class is definitely a token, not a type. (W. V. Quine has regularly spoken of classes as universals. But because classes are not repeatables, and universals are repeatables, Quine's terminology has a good deal of potentiality to mislead.)

So an electron, a token, is related, by the relation of class membership, to another token, the class of electrons. Nice work in getting rid of types. The only worry is the relation of class membership. It is a type: repeated in each case where a thing is a member of some class. But there are special reasons, which I will not go into at present, for thinking that that problem can at least be contained.

I will now turn aside and contrast this rather good situation for the Class Nominalist with the not so good situation for the Predicate Nominalist. A **Predicate Nominalist**, as I will define the term, is one who holds that for a token to be an instance of a certain type, be of a certain kind or sort, is for a certain predicate, a linguistic entity, to apply to or be true of the token. This is *literally* a Nominalist theory. To be white is for the predicate, the word 'white', to apply to the token in question.

But when we speak of the predicate 'white' here, are we speaking of a predicate token or of a predicate type? It can be thought of as a token—but not just any old token. It must be a token of the right type: the word 'white' taken as a type or, more accurately, any word that means what 'white' means in English. The Predicate Nominalist's account of the type *white* therefore makes essential reference to another type: a semantic type. He has pushed down the bulge in the carpet only to have it reappear elsewhere. But now he owes us an account of this new type. If he goes on with his Predicate Nominalism, then something being of this semantic type will be analyzed in a way that involves another, more complex, semantic type. This is to embark on an infinite regress. It appears to be vicious.

Predicate Nominalism suffers from another disadvantage by comparison with Class Nominalism. Classes are always there, whether human beings are there or not. Thus in a minimal sense Class Nominalism is a Realist theory. (We could call it a Realist Reductionism about universals.) But unlike classes, predicates may not be available. Yet there are certainly types—undiscovered scientific properties, for instance—for which no predicates (words) exist now or perhaps ever will.

The Predicate Nominalist would have to give an account of such types in terms of *possible* predicates. That gets him onto very tricky ground. What is the foundation in reality, in the world, that makes statements about possible predicates true? After all, one would not ordinarily assume that, over and above the actual predicates that we actually use, there are such things as "possible predicates." The merely possible, most of us think, does not exist. So what is the force of an account of actual types, even if they are unknown ones, in terms of possible predicates? The Predicate Nominalist will be hard-pressed to say. (For more on Predicate Nominalism see Armstrong 1978a, Chapter 2. Class Nominalism is discussed in Chapter 4 of that book.) A variant of Predicate Nominalism is **Concept Nominalism**, in which the concept, something in people's minds, is substituted for the word 'white'. This theory seems to be no worse, but no better, than the Predicate theory.

So among extreme Nominalisms I think that Class Nominalism is to be preferred to Predicate Nominalism. But even Class Nominalism is not satisfactory. Later I shall discuss other difficulties, but here I will take up one problem only: the difficulty of correlating classes and types. If Class Nominalism is a true theory, then there ought to be a one-one correlation between classes and types. But such a correlation is not to be found.

First, the Class Nominalist requires that corresponding to each type (kind, sort, property), there is a class. That seems fairly right. Maybe the type is so special that there is only one instance. But that is no problem. Set theory recognizes unit classes.

A bit more worrying are types to which *no* instances correspond: unicornhood and centaurhood, for example. Set theory does recognize the null class. But the trouble is that there is only *one* null class. If being a unicorn is identical with being a member of the null class and being a centaur is identical with being a member of the null class, then, by the transitivity and symmetry of identity, being a unicorn and being a centaur are the very same type. This seems absurd.

Types that have no instances are a bit peculiar, and perhaps in a developed theory one will not want to say that they are genuine types. Perhaps they are only *possible* types. A possible type is not necessarily a type, one could argue, any more than a possible murderer is necessarily a murderer. So let us thrust aside types that have no instances and agree, at least for the sake of argument, that to every type there corresponds a class.

But now, second, comes a really big difficulty in correlating types and classes. Is it the case that for every class there exists a type, its own special type, which has that class as its extension? (The *extension* of a type is the class of all and only the things that are tokens of that type.) There is little reason to think that you can always find such a type.

The trouble starts here from the utter ubiquity of classes. Anything whatsoever, any entity of any sort, can be put, or rather be found, in a class with any number of other things of any sort whatever. You can take the Sydney Opera House, the square root of 2, the city of Berlin, the "Barbara" syllogism, your last thought on June 6, 1988, along with indefinitely many other things, indeed an infinity of other things. It is a perfectly good class. Moreover, given such first-order classes, there are classes of classes, and so on indefinitely.

The result is that even if every type picks out a class, the class of its tokens, there is no reason to think that to every class there corresponds a type. For a short list like the preceding one you might say: Everything in it was thought about by Armstrong. Then you might find some general property of Armstrong that is rather complex and thus marks him off from everything else. Then you could say that the five things have the property of being used as philosophical examples by a being having that complex property. That can claim to be a type, a pure type, and one that generates an open class, though an extremely uninteresting one. But classes do not have to be listed. They exist whether anybody thinks of them or not. So it will not be possible to repeat such tricks for all the classes.

The only way to solve the problem would be to introduce types that are disjunctions of simpler types (type A *or* type B *or* . . . ). If you are faced with the class that contains all the ravens together with all the writing desks, then you introduce a 'type' either a raven or a writing desk. You would need to include infinite disjunctions for classes that have an infinite number of members and are infinitely variegated. But that is surely faking. There would be no genuine *unity* in such classes, thus no genuine type.

So the Class Nominalist is wrong to say that to be of a type (be a kind or sort, have a general property) is just to be a member of a class. That is certainly involved. But the type is more than that. To be a member of a class is necessary *but not sufficient* for being of a certain type. The philosopher who has most insisted upon this point is Anthony Quinton (1957 and 1973, Chapter 9).

If this has been correct, then we can formulate the Problem of Universals in the following way: *What distinguishes the classes of tokens that mark off a type from those classes that do not?* I think that this is a good way to formulate the problem. The really interesting and attractive solutions to the

Problem of Universals, I think, are those that start from this point and try to answer this question. Therefore, in the next section I will indicate briefly the main types of answer that can be given to the question. The rest of the book will be given over to probing the weaknesses and strengths of these answers.

I will be making one further, though I think minimal, assumption, which I will indicate now. I will assume (with some qualifications to be developed) that the distinction between the "good" and the "bad" classes is an *objective* distinction. That is, it is a distinction founded on a difference in the things themselves and not, say, in some different attitude that we take up to the different classes. That a certain class of tokens marks off a type is not something we determine. (Who are we to determine the nature of things?) Hence I will call the good classes the *natural* classes. It is fairly clear that the naturalness of classes admits of degree. Some classes are *more natural* than others.

### III. Theories of Natural Classes

The assumption, then, is that some classes are better than others, that there is an objective distinction in the world between natural and nonnatural classes, a distinction that admits of degree. What is the correct theory of this state of affairs?

1. *Natural classes as primitives*: The first theory that we must seriously consider is that the existence of natural classes, with their different degrees of naturalness, is a primitive, not further explicable, fact. This is an important view. However, it has only emerged relatively recently, at any rate in this particular form. The view was first formulated (as far as I know) by Anthony Quinton in the article in which he formulated the natural class problem. It is a Nominalist theory, involving tokens, classes of tokens (which are also

particulars), though it does involve a property of certain classes, a property of *naturalness* that admits of degrees.

2. *Resemblance Nominalism*: Against Quinton, you may think that it should be possible to explain what a natural class is, to penetrate into its structure. But if at the same time you do not like universals, that is, if you want to remain a Nominalist, then the thing to do is to analyze the notion of a natural class using the relation of *resemblance*. Natural classes are identified with classes of individuals where certain relations of resemblance hold between the individuals, thus making the class into a natural class.

Resemblance, on this view, has to be taken as something objectively there in the world. Only thus do we secure the objectivity of the natural classes. Furthermore, it is necessary to reject one traditional analysis of resemblance. This is the view that when things resemble, then they always have something in common, something strictly the same, identical in the strict sense. This traditional analysis is summed up in a slogan: All resemblance is partial identity.

It is clear why this traditional analysis of resemblance must be rejected by the Resemblance Nominalist. To speak of identity between the resembling things is to go over into a Universals theory. In Resemblance Nominalism, on the contrary, instead of the naturalness of classes being taken as primitive, the resemblance of the members is taken as primitive. (Although resemblance is permitted to have *degrees*.) Primitive resemblance is the unifier of the natural class. One philosopher who puts forward a worked out Resemblance Nominalism is the English philosopher H. H. Price (1953, Ch. 1).

3. *Universals*: Suppose that we do analyze resemblance in terms of identity. Then we pass over into explaining resemblance, and the unity of natural classes, in terms of universals.

One straightforward way to do this is to work with common, that is, the same, strictly identical, *properties* and *relations*. Individual things will have properties and be related to each other. These properties and relations will be universals, thus in the case of properties, more than one thing can have them, and in the case of relations, more than one pair, or triple, or quadruple, . . . of things can have them. These strict samenesses or identities will yield resemblances, which in turn will give us the natural classes. (We shall see later that even for a Universals theory, this cannot be the whole story about resemblance. But complications will have to wait.)

4. *Natural classes of tropes*: The Natural Class theory and the Resemblance theory do not admit properties and relations at the ground floor of their analyses. They face the problem of giving an account of our easy and natural talk about the properties and relations of things, yet using in the account only nonuniversals. The Realist admits properties and relations but holds that they are universals. This suggests an interesting nominalist compromise. Admit properties and relations, *but make them into particulars*. Of two billiard balls, let each have its own color, shade, mass, and so forth. If the balls are in contact on the table, and two others are at the other end of the table, let each pair have its *own* relations of adjacency. Following the U.S. philosopher, Donald C. Williams, we can call properties and relations conceived of as particulars tropes.

This stand does not solve the Problem of Universals, but it does allow the problem to be posed anew. Consider all the red things. On the trope theory the redness of each thing is a distinct trope. But then we have to face the question, Why do we say that all red tropes have the *same* color? The identity is not strict identity. So what unifies the class of all rednesses?

Three answers stand out once again. The first is the natural class answer. The individual rednesses form a closely unified natural class and that is all that can be said. This nominalist view was put forward by G. F. Stout. He said that the class of the rednesses have a "distributive unity." It is a trope version of Quinton's view that natural classes are primitive. But we will see later that the trope version is in many ways quite a new game (and a superior one).

5. *Resemblance classes of tropes*: Another way of uniting classes of tropes is to appeal, as a primitive, to the relation of resemblance, but now between tropes, not ordinary things. Individual rednesses resemble each other to a greater or lesser degree. This form of Resemblance Nominalism was upheld by Donald Williams. I am inclined to think that it is the most plausible of all forms of Nominalism. It is a very moderate form of Nominalism, just as the Realism I will defend later is a rather moderate form of Realism.

6. *Tropes plus universals*: Finally, one might seek to unify the class of rednesses, say, in a realist manner. Each particular redness, each trope, instantiates the single universal. This view has been held by some good philosophers, for instance, the Oxford philosopher J. Cook Wilson. It may even have been Aristotle's view. But I think it is of less interest than the first five positions. Once one has accepted universals, the tropes seem to become redundant (or vice versa).

We may set out the six theories in a 3 x 2 matrix:

|  | Ordinary Particulars | Tropes |  |
|---|---|---|---|
| Primitive Natural Classes | **1** A. Quinton | **4** G. F. Stout | ⎫ Nominalists |
| Resemblance | **2** H. H. Price | **5** D. C. Williams | ⎬ |
| Universals | **3** Plato, Aristotle(?) | **6** J. Cook Wilson | Realists |

*This diagram sets our agenda.* These, I claim, are the most plausible candidates for solutions to the Problem of Universals. We will look at each in turn, or at least the first five, considering for each its strengths and its weaknesses.

To finish the section, let us illustrate the six positions by considering how each would deal with the property of whiteness.

1. Primitive natural class view: The class of all the white things forms a natural class, a class with a reasonable degree of naturalness. That is all that can be said about what makes a white thing white.
2. Resemblance Nominalism: The white things form a natural class in virtue of the objective fact that they all resemble each other to a certain degree. Resemblance is an objective but unanalyzable fact.
3. Universals: All white things have an identical property in common (or a set of slightly different properties to correspond to the different shades of white).
4. Natural classes of tropes: Each white thing has its *own*, entirely distinct, property of whiteness. But the class of the whitenesses forms a primitive natural class.
5. Resemblance classes of tropes: Each white thing has its own property of whiteness. But the members of the class of the whitenesses all resemble each other more or less closely, with resemblance a primitive.
6. Tropes plus universals: Each white thing has its own property of whiteness. But these particular properties themselves each have a universal property of whiteness.

## IV. Methodology

Before ending this chapter it is appropriate for me to say something about method. In examining the various positions that one might take up in regard to the "natural class problem," I will be considering quite a number of arguments for and against the different positions and will be trying to assess the worth of these arguments. Argument is the life blood of any philosophical investigation that aspires to any rigor. Yet at the same time it is important not to overestimate the power of argument, even in cases where the argument is quite a good one.

Suppose that the conclusion of an argument is unwelcome. Arguments proceed from premisses, and sometimes the premisses can be questioned. Quite often, arguments are not conclusive, in the sense that there is no actual contradiction in upholding the premisses and denying the conclusion. Such arguments may point in a certain direction, but they may not *force* one in that direction. If one does not like the direction then one can "tough it out." Finally, even if it is agreed that the premisses are true and the reasoning from the premisses conclusive or reasonably conclusive, it may be possible simply to accept the conclusions. Even if the conclusions are quite unpleasant, it is often possible and may be rational to agree with the conclusions and tough it out once more. Again and again in philosophy all these maneuvres are live options.

What is to be done in this somewhat unsatisfactory situation? We have to accept, I think, that straight refutation (or proof) of a view in philosophy is rarely possible. What has to be done is to build a case against, or to build a case for, a position. One does this, usually, by examining many different arguments and considerations against and for a position and comparing them with what can be said against and for alternative views. What one should hope to arrive at, and what I try to arrive at in this book, is something like an intellectual cost-benefit analysis of the views considered.

This will not be a royal road to agreement: There is no such road in philosophy. But an attempt to provide a cost-benefit analysis, subjective though much of the assessment will be, is likely to be the best way to advance the debate.

One important way in which different philosophical and scientific theories about the same topic may be compared is in respect of intellectual economy. In general, the theory that explains the phenomena by means of the least number of entities and principles (in particular, by the least number of *sorts* of entities and principles) is to be preferred. This principle of method, which may be summed up by saying that entities are not to be postulated without necessity, is known as Occam's razor, after the medieval philosopher William of Occam, although this formulation is not actually found in his works. Philosophers will often be found appealing to the principle, particularly philosophers with empiricist or reductionist sympathies.

For this reason I will pay a certain amount of attention to how economical or uneconomical various theories are. *Other things being equal,* I shall account the more economical theory the better theory. A final section in each chapter will be addressed to giving a list of the fundamental entities and principles required by the theory examined in that chapter.

# CHAPTER TWO

# Primitive
# Natural Classes

## I. How Is It Determined that a Class Is Natural?

We start, then, by examining the view that although individual things, particulars, tokens, fall naturally into all sorts of classes and thus may be said to be of this or that type, this fact cannot be analyzed further. It is a primitive, or ground-floor, feature of the world that there are such classes, classes that, in G. F. Stout's nice phrase, have a "distributive unity," and have this unity in different degrees. It is a matter of the degree of close-knittedness of the class. This is an important view, but if we exclude Stout it has only been explicitly put forward by one philosopher: Anthony Quinton. (Stout is excluded for the present because, unlike Quinton, he admitted properties and relations into his ground-floor entities. These properties and relations he conceived of as particulars, not universals, and he formed his natural classes from such things as all the particular rednesses.)

How does one determine that a certain class of things is a natural class? Quinton thinks of the matter in a way that is indebted to Wittgenstein. Suppose that one has been presented

It is suggested that Anthony Quinton's paper "Properties and Classes" be used as a companion reading to this chapter.

(perhaps as a child) with various specimens of blue objects, including all different shades and varieties of the color so as to give the full spread of the word 'blue' across the color spectrum. If one is then able, with relative ease, to identify individuals that one has never met before as belonging in the same class with the original objects, then this shows that the class of blue things is a *natural* class.

It can be seen from this that Quinton's notion of a natural class is in part an epistemological notion. That is to say, it ties the naturalness of a class to what we find natural to take together as a class. There is something right about this, because this is where we have to start in determining that certain classes are natural. How could one start except with certain classifications that we naturally make? But I do not think that the process of searching out the true natural classes *ends* there.

What enterprise is it that tries to determine what natural classes there are in the world? It is the enterprise of natural science. One thing that the natural sciences further try to do is to establish the large-scale geography and history of the universe. But they do much more. They try to establish just what sorts of things there are in the world, in particular, what are the more fundamental sorts of things, the things in terms of which all other sorts of things are explained. The sciences further try to establish the properties and relations that the sorts of things have. (They also, and this is very important, try to establish the *laws* that the sorts obey. But that is not our present concern.) We can put this establishing of the sorts in the language of the Natural Class theory. The natural sciences are trying to establish just what the *true* natural classes are. In Plato's wonderful metaphor, they are trying to carve the beast of reality along the joints.

But if it is up to the natural sciences to determine what are the true natural classes, then it is clear that what we begin by accepting as the natural classes—the classifications that we make in the state of nature before organized inquiry has gone to work: Quinton's classes—are only a first stab at the natural classes. There are natural classes that we eventually come to accept, but that we would never have dreamed about before science started its work, for instance, the class of the electrons. Some of the classes that we begin by regarding as closely knit natural classes may have to be shoved down the class ladder and replaced by other classes much more theoretically arrived at. For a very simple example, remember that the class of fish once included whales. Later, in the interest of a tighter organization that carved nearer the joints, whales were excluded.

We start with what Wilfrid Sellars (1963, Ch. 1) calls "the manifest image" of the world. (Roughly, Quinton's natural classes.) We try to break through to what Sellars calls the "scientific image" of the world (the true natural classes). In the course of so doing we not only greatly amplify, greatly expand, the manifest image, but we also find reason to *criticize* it. We cannot overthrow the manifest image completely. It is where we start from in conducting our observations. Our scientific theories are tested against observation, and at the very minimum the theories must explain satisfactorily why our manifest image is as it is. But we do have to go beyond the manifest image. From the point of view of the theory of natural classes, we are replacing the classes of the first look, the classes that Quinton appeals to, with a more sophisticated and deeper classification.

My suggestion, in short, is that a Natural Class theory is best put forward in a *scientific realist* form.

## II. Degrees of Naturalness

It is a very important point, and one emphasized by Quinton, that although the naturalness of a class is for him a primitive notion, nevertheless it admits of degrees. That is to say, one natural class may be more closely knit, more of a unity, than another natural class. Consider the difference between the class of the colored things and the class of the crimson things.

Both are natural classes. But the latter is much more closely knit, has a much higher degree of unity, than has the class of the colored things.

The class of the crimson things is actually contained within the class of the colored things. This helps to make the difference in degree of unity of the two classes a clear-cut matter. But often the ranking of natural classes in terms of degrees of unity is a bit rough-and-ready, not to say arbitrary and conventional. How do you compare the class of earthquakes with the class of volcanic eruptions with respect to their unity? The ranking of natural classes in terms of degrees of unity is a bit like ranking societies by how free they are. In both sorts of case you can make some sort of ranking. But the ranking will very often not be all that precise and definite.

Notice, however, that the unity scale for natural classes appears to have a top. If there is a plurality of things all exactly alike, perfect twins, then the class has the highest possible degree of unity. So the scale is not like the number series, where there is always a higher number. Whether this top is actually realized is an empirical question. It is not realized at the macroscopic level but may obtain at the level of fundamental physical particles.

The number series does have a lowest number: 0. The natural class scale also seems to have a bottom limit. These are the classes that are utterly heterogeneous, having no unity at all: the *non*natural classes.

These characteristics of the natural class scale are rather unsatisfactory from the point of view of the Natural Class theory. Naturalness of class is supposed to be a primitive, but we have just noticed that it is a rather messy primitive. Naturalness admits of degrees, with a highest and lowest degree, although perhaps the two limits are never reached. Still worse, the ordering of classes by degree seems a vague and spotty affair, involving arbitrary decisions. It is natural to think that behind degrees of naturalness lies some more precise notion. In later chapters we shall see the Resemblance theory trying to explicate the notion of a natural class in terms of resemblances between the members of the class, resemblances that admit of degree. The Universals theory seeks to go still further and analyze even the fact of resemblance.

## III. The Coextension Problem

Coextensive properties are properties possessed by the very same class of things. Quine's often-mentioned example is that of being a cordate (having a heart) and being a renate (having kidneys). All creatures that have hearts have kidneys, and vice versa. But it seems that a Natural Class Nominalist (or, indeed, any Class Nominalist) cannot admit coextensive properties.

One natural class can be a *subset* of another; for instance, the class of crimson things is a subset of the class of colored things. One natural class can *intersect* with another; for instance, the class of elephants and the class of male animals intersect. But two different natural classes cannot *coincide* because two different classes cannot coincide. Classes that coincide are the very same class.

Quine says that the identity conditions for classes are "crystal clear." Classes are identical if and only if their members are identical. Contemporary philosophers all accept these identity conditions for classes. Indeed, they take these conditions to hold by definition. So given any class analysis of what it is to be of a certain type (be of a certain sort or kind, have a certain property), then it will be impossible for one class of tokens to be the class for more than one type. There cannot be coextensive types.

But coextensive types certainly seem to be possible. Suppose that surfaces are red if and only if they answer to a certain physical formula having to do with the emission of light waves. A physicalist (such as myself) might take it that this formula tells us what redness *is*. Against this, however, might it not be the case that redness is distinct from the physical property of the surface, although exactly correlated with it? But if a class analysis of types is correct, then this position can be ruled out a priori. (It is quite likely that, for reasons given by Saul Kripke, this possibility is no more than what philosophers call a mere *doxastic* possibility: something conceivable, but not genuinely possible. However, that does not destroy the force of the example.)

It is interesting to look at the position of David Lewis here. Lewis is a **modal realist**, believing in the literal existence of innumerable possible worlds over and above our own (see Lewis 1986a). He is also attracted to, without definitely endorsing, a Natural Class theory (see Lewis 1983 and 1986b). Lewis has a way of dealing with the coextension problem. His natural classes range over every possible world, not merely our actual world. Suppose then that two properties are coextensive in this world. Provided that it is just a *contingent* fact that properties are coextensive, then there will be possible worlds in which some things have one of the properties but not the other. In our world all cordates are renates and all renates are cordates. But this seems contingent only. So there will exist possible worlds containing cordates that are not renates, and worlds containing renates that are not cordates. Thus for Lewis the two natural classes will be different. The properties are not coextensive across all possible worlds.

Lewis would still be in trouble if there are cases where two distinct properties are *necessarily* coextensive, because what is necessary holds in *all* possible worlds. The obvious reply would be to argue that in such an alleged case the necessary connection shows that the supposed two properties are really only one. But this reply may be in difficulty. Elliott Sober (1982) has argued that the properties of being a three-sided plane figure and being a three-angled plane figure (being trilateral and being triangular) are distinct, but necessarily coextensive, properties.

## IV. Wolterstorff's Argument from the Identity Conditions of Classes

The next three arguments are all close cousins of each other. Perhaps they are the same argument at bottom. I begin with the argument advanced by Nicholas Wolterstorff in his book *On Universals* (1970, Ch. 8).

A class, as Quine says, is determined by its members. Change its membership and it is automatically a different class. Consider then the view that to be an electron, say, is to be a member of the class of electrons. These electrons are contingent beings. That is to say, some or all of them might not have existed. Other electrons besides the ones that exist might have existed. In that case, as Quine's point indicates, we would have been dealing with a different class. But given a class analysis of what it is to be an electron, a change in the membership of the class entails that the type *being an electron* would have been different. This is a clear consequence of the class analysis. But is it an acceptable consequence? It seems not. Intuitively, given these changes in class membership, *being an electron* would not have been, certainly need not have been, any different. Electron nature is independent of electron class.

Once again David Lewis can escape this consequence, though at the cost of postulating all those possible worlds. His natural class of electrons is the class that has as members all the electrons in all possible worlds. *This* class could not be other than it is. Every possibility for electrons is exhausted. So Wolterstorff could not get his argument going against Lewis.

## V. Types Determine Classes, Not Classes Types

Consider the following question. Is a thing the sort of thing that it is—an electron, say—*because* it is a member of the class of electrons? Or is it rather a member of the class *because* it is an electron? It is a matter of deciding what is the **direction of explanation.** Compare Socrates' question to Euthyphro, in Plato's dialogue *Euthyphro.* Are pious acts pious *because* they are loved by the gods? That is, is being loved by the gods what constitutes their being pious? Or do the gods love these acts *because* of their piety? Or again, is what constitutes a thing's beauty that it is admired aesthetically? Or is it admired aesthetically because it is beautiful?

Whatever we say about piety and beauty, notoriously difficult questions, it seems natural to say that a thing is a member of the class of electrons because of what it *already* is: an electron. It is unnatural to say that it is an electron because it is a member of the class of electrons. And that it is natural to put the property first and the class second is some reason to think that that is the true direction of explanation. This is bad news for any Class Nominalism. If type determines class membership, then class membership cannot determine type.

## VI. The Causal Argument

When things act causally, they act in virtue of their properties. The object depresses the scales in virtue of its mass; the fire makes the water boil in virtue of its temperature; and so on. But suppose that we try to give an account of a thing's properties in terms of classes of which it is a member. The object acts in virtue of the fact that it has a mass of four kilograms. But it is that individual four-kilogram object that acts. The other four-kilogram things in the universe seem to be irrelevant. However, if a class analysis of what it is to be four kilograms in mass is correct, then the whole class of tokens should be relevant: The four-kilo property of the individual is constituted by its class membership. But in fact, though, the only thing relevant is the thing that actually acts. This suggests that any class account of properties is unsatisfactory.

In order to bring out the force of this argument, consider the situation where we perceive a new token of a familiar type. Suppose that we have no difficulty in classifying it as being of that type. Surely what has happened is that the object has *acted* on us, causing us to classify it correctly. But it does not just act on us, it acts in virtue of certain properties. Take the simplest case and let the situation be one where the cause is a thing's having a certain property, the thing's being red, say, and the effect is that we recognize the thing to have that very property. Now, on the Natural Class theory these properties are *constituted* by the token's being a member of a certain class, perhaps a huge, even infinite, class. How does this relation of an individual red token to the whole class of red things get into the causal act? It is not easy to see.

## VII. The Problem About Relations

We now come to a very important question for the Natural Class theory. What account is it to give of **relations**?

Philosophy has been a long time coming to grips with the category of relation. Aristotle said of relations that they were "least of all things a kind of entity or substance" (*Metaphysics* 1088 a 22). The tradition has tended to echo this ever since. The categories of substance (thing) and attribute (property) are long established, but not so the category of relation. It is not until the late nineteenth and the twentieth century with C. S. Peirce, William James, and Bertrand Russell that relations begin (no more than begin) to come into focus.

The question for the Natural Class theory is what to do with relation types: *being to the left of,* and so on. It will not do to gather together all the things between which this relation holds into a single class and declare that class natural. The best that that would do would give us a *property* for each member of the class. The *relation* would be lost. What seems to be needed instead is *classes of classes.* Let us start with something that will prove too simple and try to work up.

Suppose that the relation is *precedes* (in time), which is a dyadic or two-term relation. First we take all the cases of individuals where one precedes the other, and we put each pair into a class by itself. We will have $\{a, b\}$, $\{c, d\}$, $\{a, d\}$, ..., and so on indefinitely. Now we form a class out of these classes, that is, a class having these classes as its members (a second-order class):

$$\{\{a, b\}, \{c, d\}, \{a, d\}, \ldots\}.$$

This second-order class seems a quite good candidate for a natural class. We could symbolize this by using the predicate letter N. Then we have:

$$N \{\{a, b\}, \{c, d\}, \{a, d\}, \ldots\},$$

which asserts of this big class that it is natural. Similarly,

$$\{a, b\} \in \{\{a, b\}, \{c, d\}, \{a, d\}, \ldots\}$$

asserts that the pair $a, b$ is a member of the big class ($\in$ is the symbol for class membership). Could this be the natural class analysis of *a precedes b*?

Unfortunately, this treatment is too simple. It will work for symmetrical relations such as being a mile apart. But it will not be adequate for asymmetrical relations such as precedes or nonsymmetrical relations such as loves.

What we have been using up to this point, according to the standard symbolism, are *unordered* classes. For unordered classes, $\{a, b\}$ is identical with $\{b, a\}$. The order of the symbols makes no difference. And if one is dealing with a symmetrical relation, there will be no problem. $a$'s being a mile from $b$ seems to be the very same thing as $b$'s being a mile from $a$. But the American Revolution's preceding the French Revolution is a very different thing from the French Revolution's preceding the American Revolution. So is Jim's loving Mary and Mary's loving Jim. The *unordered* classes (the American Revolution, the French Revolution) and (Jim, Mary) completely lose this information.

What is needed in this situation is what set theorists call *ordered* pairs (triples, quadruples, . . . , n-tuples), where the order of the symbols inside the class symbols *is* significant. The ordered class $<a, b>$ is *not* identical with $<b, a>$. The Natural Class theory can then analyze $a$'s preceding $b$ as a situation where the ordered class $<a, b>$ is a member of the unordered (but natural) class of ordered pairs $\{<a, b>, <c, d>, <a, d>, . . .\}$. The ordered pairs are all the pairs of entities where the first member of the pair precedes the second member in time.

How satisfactory is this device of ordered pairs? Notice that the notion of *order* is the notion of a certain sort of relation, and a quite complex relation at that. So the best that would have been done by the analysis is to reduce all the different sorts of relation to a single, and complex, sort of relation. Relations would not have been eliminated entirely.

However, logicians do have a way of getting rid of ordered pairs (triples, etc.). It is called the Wiener-Kuratowski device, because it was proposed independently by these two logicians. What is done is to substitute for the ordered pair $<a, b>$ the *unordered* pair of unordered classes:

$$\{\{a\}, \{a, b\}\}.$$

This serves as a formal substitute for order. The thing $a$ is put in a class by itself—what is called a unit class. This creates an asymmetry between $a$ and $b$ and thus enables us to order them, even though nothing is used except unordered classes. The natural class of pairs of things where the first precedes the second can then be taken to be a huge unordered class containing all these unordered classes of classes as members.

But I am inclined to think that the difference between

31

<a, b> and {{a}, {a, b}} is really of minor importance. The fundamental difficulty is that although these classes may be fitted to *represent* a relation between *a* and *b*, yet they do not seem to *be* that relation. This holds even where these classes are embedded in natural classes and full weight is given to the embedding in fixing the nature of the relation between *a* and *b*.

<a, b> is to be *a*'s preceding *b*. But why should it not be *a*'s *succeeding* *b*? No objection, the set theorist will reply, provided that in the one stretch of discourse or calculation you always stick to the same rule. The first term in each ordered pair must always be the predecessor, or else it must always be the successor. Similarly for the class of classes construction of Wiener and Kuratowski.

But does this not suggest very strongly that we are in the presence of mere representations? Either *a* precedes *b* or else *a* succeeds *b*. Yet either of these possible states of affairs can be represented, mapped, by either of the formulas <a, b> and <b, a>, or else by either of {{a}, {a, b}} and {{b}, {a, b}}. The Class Nominalist, however, has *identified* relations with classes of objects. So all that he has got in the world is <a, b> and <b, a> or else {{a}, {a, b}} and {{b}, {a, b}}. But if it is arbitrary which of these constitutes *a*'s preceding *b* and which *a*'s succeeding *b*, has not the clear-cut difference between *a*'s preceding *b* and *a*'s succeeding *b* leaked away?

## VIII. Higher-Order Types

In the first chapter I drew the almost pretheoretical distinction between tokens and types. However, types may themselves be tokens falling under higher-order types. For instance, being red, green, yellow, and so forth, are all types, but at the same time they are each of them tokens falling under the higher-order type *color*. Each of them is a color. Quantities yield important cases of this sort, especially important for a

Scientific Realist. Consider properties like having a mass of one ton, one pound, one kilogram. These types can all be brought under a single type: mass properties.

As well as bringing types under a single type, we also appear to have relations between types. Consider the fact that redness is more like orange than it is like yellow, or that blue is more like purple than it is like red. Here a three-term relation of being more like than connects triples that are types. Similar orderings of types may be found within the quantities. One kilogram in mass is between one pound in mass and one ton in mass. Laws of nature also seem to involve relations between types. Newton's law of gravitation, $G = (M_1 \times M_2)/D^2$, relates gravitational attraction between bodies to the product of their masses divided by the square of their distance. Here we seem to have a *functional relation* between ranges of types.

Any solution to the Problem of Universals must be able to deal with higher-order types and the relations of types. How does the Natural Class theory fare? When a type is brought under a type, the type redness under the type color, for instance, then it is obvious that this has implications for the tokens that fall under the first-order type. Because redness is a color, all red things are colored. This raises the hope that one may be able to reduce all statements about higher-order types to statements about first-order tokens. Given such reductions, the Natural Class theorist could then easily put the reductions into class form.

So we take:

(1)     Redness is a color.

We translate it as:

(1')     Each red thing is a colored thing.

This would in turn translate into the language of natural classes as:

33

(1'')  The natural class of red things is a subclass of the natural class of colored things.

There is no doubt that (1) entails the truth of (1') and (1''). If the entailment goes the other way also, then we could hope that we had found a good reductive analysis of (1).

A second example involves bringing three types under the three-term relation *more like than*:

(2)  Redness is more like orange than it is like yellow.

For this we could try:

(2')  For all $x$, all $y$, and all $z$, if $x$ is red, $y$ is orange, and $z$ is yellow, then $x$ is more like $y$ than $x$ is like $z$.

I will not bother to put this in the language of natural classes.

Unfortunately, however, (1') and (2') are not satisfactory translations. To see that this is so consider first:

(1''')  Each red thing is an extended thing.

As Frank Jackson has pointed out (1977), this has the very same form as (1'). It even resembles (1') in apparently being a necessary truth. Yet no one would conclude from (1''') that redness is an extension. It is not—it is a color. This shows that (1')—each red thing is a colored thing—*undertranslates* red is a color. You need a closer connection between redness and color than that provided by (1').

It is even clearer that (2') is not a satisfactory translation of red is more like orange than it is like yellow. Suppose that $x$ is a red car, $y$ is a ripe orange, and $z$ is a yellow car of exactly the same make as the red one. Surely $x$ is more like $z$ than it is like the orange? This means that (2') is not even true: It is a universal proposition that is false for certain values of $x, y,$ and $z$. So it cannot be a satisfactory translation of (2), which is true. (This was pointed out by Arthur Pap 1959.)

So the Natural Class theory will have to deal with higher-order types in some other way. The obvious thing to try is higher-order natural classes: natural classes of natural classes. Red things form a natural class, so do the blue things, and so on. Perhaps to say that red is a color is to say that the natural class of red things is a member of a certain natural class of natural classes. One could then go on to say that red is more like orange than it is like yellow is to be analyzed in the following way. There is a natural class of classes whose members are the class of red things and the class of orange things. There is another natural class of classes whose members are the class of red things and the class of yellow things. But the first class of classes is more natural than the second:

{{red things}, {orange things}} $>_N$ {{red things}, {yellow things}}

where $>_N$ is to be read as "is more natural than."

But this second analysis, at least, is not satisfactory. It would fail if red things and orange things were very unalike in their *other* characteristics, while red things and yellow things were very alike in their other characteristics. The class of the red things and the class of the yellow things would then go together more naturally in a class of classes than the class of the red things and the class of the orange things. (Let the only red things be elephants, the only yellow things be rhinoceroses, and the only orange things be ripe oranges.) It does not matter that we have to make false suppositions about the nature of the world to falsify the analysis. For it is clear that even in an imaginary world, the color red would still be more like orange than it is like yellow.

In general, it seems likely that the Natural Class theory cannot explain the ordering of properties. That is a most serious shortcoming, particularly in view of the pressing need to explain the systematic ordering of quantities: masses, lengths, and so on.

## IX. The Apparatus of the Natural Class Theory

Finally, let us look at the apparatus that the Natural Class theory needs to postulate and see what difficulties, if any, there are as a result. First, the Natural Class theory is a *class* theory. Besides individuals, first-order tokens, the theory requires classes, including classes of higher order. I do not think that this is any reproach to the natural class view. Classes have turned out to be rather mysterious entities in modern metaphysics; nobody seems to have got a firm grip on their nature. But set theory is a well-established discipline whose truth we can hardly deny. This means that we must admit either that there are such things as classes or at least that statements about classes have definite truth conditions. (Statements about the average taxpayer have definite truth conditions although there is no thing that is the average taxpayer.) That should be good enough for the Natural Class theory.

Second, the Natural Class theory does require the *relation* of class membership holding between individuals and classes of individuals. It may be thought that here is a difficulty for the theory, because it analyzes relations in terms of classes (see Sec. VII of this chapter). Applied to the relation of class membership itself, the analysis has to use $\in$, the relation in question, in the course of giving an analysis of $\in$.

I used to think that that was a difficulty for class theories (see Armstrong 1978a, Ch. 4, Sec. VII). However, I now believe that the difficulty can be got around. But I will defer discussion of this until Chapter 3, Section XI.

We pass on, then, third, to the notion of *natural* class. Here we strike a prima facie problem. Naturalness of class appears to be a *property* of classes—an unanalyzable property according to the theory, although it admits of degrees—a property that is a universal because many different classes all have it. Does the theory have to admit one universal here?

Perhaps a first step to meeting the difficulty is the following: We divide all classes whose members involve first-level individuals (tokens) only, into two sorts. First, there are classes that are totally heterogeneous: those that have no naturalness at all (0 on the naturalness scale). Second, there are classes that have some positive degree of naturalness. This second lot form a class: the class of all the natural classes. Now can we not say that this higher-order class is natural? And then we can suggest that what it is for each of the particular natural classes to be natural is simply for them to be members of this (super)natural class. It is true that we are left with a primitive—the naturalness of this big class of classes—that it seems we must treat as a property and take as a primitive in the theory. But it is not a universal, for it is not something repeated or repeatable.

This is only a first step, because there is still an account to be given of degrees of naturalness. One class may be more natural than another, less natural, or equally natural. These relations between classes will presumably have to be dealt with in the same way that the theory deals with relations between ordinary particulars. We saw in Section VII that relations constitute a difficulty for the Natural Class theory, but at least it can be argued here that relations between classes introduce no *new* difficulty of principle.

Fourth, and finally, the *formal* properties of naturalness of class are part of the cost of the theory. We noted in Section II that axioms for naturalness are required: in particular, that naturalness has a highest and a lowest degree. There is also the point that the assigning of intermediate degrees is a rough-and-ready, somewhat arbitrary, affair. (We compared such a ranking to the possible but loose ranking of societies in terms of the degrees of freedom that they enjoy.) These properties of naturalness of class have no further explanation. So they are part of the cost of the theory.

We have uncovered various difficulties for the Natural Class theory: the coextension problem, the way properties are naturally taken not to vary with the class of things having that property, the problem about relations, and the problem of higher-order types. All these problems would perhaps be solved (although others might be created) if the theory could only admit properties and relations. Nor would this involve abandoning Nominalism if properties and relations were admitted as particulars only (tropes).

Without properties and relations, individual objects are relatively structureless. Without properties and relations they can still have parts and be parts of larger wholes, and these parts may perhaps include temporal as well as the less controversial spatial parts. (You yesterday as a temporal part of you.) I therefore call the Natural Class theory, in the form that is put forward by Quinton, a Blob theory. The next theory to be examined, orthodox Resemblance Nominalism, is also a blob theory. By contrast, theories that admit properties and relations, whether as universals or particulars, may be called Layer-cake theories. For myself, I believe that they have substantial advantages over blob theories.

It is economical to try and get along without properties and relations. But I think it is a false economy. Blob theories do not give things enough structure.

# CHAPTER THREE

# Resemblance Nominalism

## I. Properties of Resemblance

At this point we turn to a theory that is also a Nominalist theory, but that tries to *analyze* the notion of a natural class. The Natural Class theory treats the naturalness of a class as an overall or, as it were, a gestalt property of the class. The Resemblance theory, however, tries to analyze this property in terms of resemblance relations holding between the individual members of the class, in terms of what John Locke called "the similitudes between things." This looks attractive. If naturalness is broken down into a multitude of resemblance relations, in many cases involving resemblances of different degrees, that might explain why degree of naturalness is a rather rough-and-ready or even indeterminate measure.

Resemblance has certain formal properties, which it is important to appreciate. As already mentioned, resemblance is like naturalness of class in admitting of degrees. Also like naturalness, there is a theoretical upper limit of exact resemblance and a theoretical lower limit of no resemblance at all. Notice that only if *each* member of a class exactly

---

It is suggested that Chapter 1 of H. H. Price's *Thinking and Experience* be used as a companion reading to this chapter.

resembles every other member of that class do we get a natural class with the highest possible degree of unity.

We should perhaps take quick and unfavorable notice of the view sometimes encountered that degrees of resemblance are quite arbitrary because with respect to any two things at all we can find an indefinite number of resemblances and an indefinite number of differences and that as a result, no two things are in themselves more, or less, alike than any other two. To take this view is really to go back to the view that there are no objective natural classes. It seems to depend upon quite gerrymandered resemblances and differences, perhaps using wildly disjunctive predicates. But it is not the case that ravens have any resemblance to writing desks just because both fall under the one predicate "either a raven or a writing desk"! We will, then, continue to assume that there are objective degrees of resemblance.

Resemblance to a particular degree, to degree D say, is symmetrical. If $a$ resembles $b$ to degree D, then $b$ resembles $a$ to just that degree. If you resemble your sister quite closely, then your sister resembles you to just that same degree. But resemblance to degree D is not *transitive*. If $a$ resembles $b$ to degree D, and if $b$ resembles $c$ to the same degree, then it by no means follows that $a$ resembles $c$ to degree D. If you resemble your sister quite closely and your sister resembles your mother quite closely, it is perfectly possible that you have no close resemblance to your mother. Intuitively, this is because of the possibility that the pair $\{a, b\}$ (you and your sister) and the pair $\{b, c\}$ (your sister and your mother) resemble each other in different respects. Perhaps you and your sister resemble quite closely only in respect of looks, while your sister and your mother resemble quite closely only in respect of character. But talk about respects is dangerous talk for the Resemblance theory. It suggests an analysis of resemblance in terms of common (identical) features in the resembling things, common features that may differ from case to case. But that is the Realist theory, the Universals theory. The

Resemblance theory takes resemblance to be an unanalyzable primitive.

You do get transitivity in one special case: at the highest point in the scale. If *a* resembles *b* exactly and *b* resembles *c* exactly, then *a* resembles *c* exactly. If you are exactly like somebody else and that somebody else is exactly like a third person, then you must be exactly like that third person. This is an instance of a more general principle that will later prove to be of great importance. If *a* resembles *b* to degree D, then this degree of resemblance is always preserved if exactly resembling things are substituted for either *a* or *b*. If you resemble another person quite closely, then you will have exactly the same degree of resemblance to that person's identical twin.

Returning to exact resemblance, it is convenient to say that the relation is *reflexive*, that is, that everything exactly resembles itself. Suppose that there exist two exactly resembling things. By symmetry we have both *a* exactly resembles *b*, and *b* exactly resembles *a*. But then by transitivity applied to the formulas in the previous sentence, we have *a* exactly resembles *a*.

I said "it is convenient to say" that exact resemblance is reflexive because I doubt whether much hangs on the claim. But it satisfies the demands of logicians, who say that if and only if a relation is symmetrical, transitive, and reflexive, then it picks out a very important sort of class: an equivalence class.

The interest of an equivalence class is that by means of its equivalence relation R, it divides up everything between which R holds (the field of R) into mutually exclusive classes of objects, classes without any members in common. Inside each equivalence class each member has R to every other member, but fails to have R to any other object. Thus because exact resemblance is an equivalence relation, it divides up the field of things that exactly resemble each other into mutually exclusive bundles. In this respect, it behaves like a universal without being one.

It might be thought that it is not very important that exact resemblance is an equivalence relation, because there are relatively few things, if any, that exactly resemble each other. But although the matter is not of immediate importance to us, there are some controversial entities between which, if they exist at all, exact resemblance is *not* an uncommon affair. These entities are properties and relations taken as particulars, what we have agreed to call tropes. For instance, the color trope associated with object *a* might exactly resemble the distinct color trope associated with distinct object *b*. Similarly for relation tropes, such as being one mile distant from, which hold between many pairs of objects. Equivalence classes of exactly resembling tropes, we shall see in Chapter 6, make very interesting *substitutes* for universals.

We may think of the various rules that we have met with in this section as Axioms of Resemblance that govern the notion of resemblance.

A final point before concluding the section: We have already noticed that the Natural Class theory must take the notion of degrees of naturalness as a primitive notion, but that the ordering of classes in such degrees is an imprecise affair (Chapter 2, Section II). Such an imprecise primitive is not very attractive.

The Resemblance theory analyzes the notion of a natural class in terms of networks of resemblance relations holding between the members of the class, relations that also admit of degree. But how precise are degrees of resemblance? We have rejected the idea that degrees of resemblance are quite arbitrary. But suppose that *a* and *b* resemble each other to a certain degree and that the same holds for *c* and *d*. I may be quite clear that *a* resembles *b* more than *c* resembles *d*. But will it be the case that for *any* pair of pairs, the first pair resembles more closely than the second pair, or resembles less closely, or resembles to the same degree? It seems rather implausible. Like naturalness of class, degree of resemblance seems to be a somewhat spotty and imprecise matter. As the logicians say, it sets up a partial ordering only. This is not a very attractive feature of the resemblance relation from the point of view of a Resemblance Nominalist. It may suggest that resemblance is not primitive but can be given some further analysis.

## II. That Resemblance Is an Internal Relation and the Consequences of This

A very important further fact about resemblance is that it is an *internal* rather than an *external* relation. Different philosophers seem to have had different things in mind when they spoke of internal and external relations, and in any case the definitions need to be formulated with some care. The distinction I have in mind was already made by Hume, although he had a clumsy terminology of "relations of ideas" (internal) and "relations of matters of fact" (external) (*Treatise*, Bk. 1, Pt. 1, Sec. V, and Pt. III, Sec. I).

A relation is internal, as I shall use the term, when given certain terms with certain natures, the relation must hold between the terms. It holds "in every possible world" that contains these terms and where these terms have these natures. With an external relation there is no such necessity. Given the numbers 4 and 2 as terms, then it follows, given the nature of 4 and 2, that they stand in the relation of greater and less. "4 is greater than 2" therefore expresses an internal relation holding between these numbers. Contrast the case where *a* is a mile distant from *b*. In general, the existence of *a* and *b* and their natures fail to ensure that *a* is a mile distant from *b*. It is a contingent matter, not holding in every possible world, that *a* is a mile from *b*. (In general, spatiotemporal and causal relations are external. Of course, one could take 'nature' so widely that being a mile from *b* was counted as part of the nature of *a*. With nature so defined one would have an— uninteresting—case of an internal relation.)

I think it is clear (and was recognized by Hume) that

resemblance is an internal relation. Given that two objects each have a certain nature, then their resemblance and its degrees are fixed. There is no possible world in which the objects remain unaltered but in which their degree of resemblance changes. Contrast this with distance. There is a possible world in which the objects remain unaltered but their distance from each other is changed. (Provided, of course, that 'altered' is not given so wide a sense as to include that very relation of distance.) Distance, therefore, is external.

Resemblance Nominalists seem not to have thought enough about the consequences of resemblance's being an internal relation. (Neither had I, until quite recently.) As we have just seen, it is the mark of an internal, as opposed to an external, relation that the terms and their nature dictate the relation. A question that then arises for the Resemblance Nominalist is, what is it about the nature that determines the resemblance? A very natural answer is that the resemblance is dictated by common properties of the related things. But the Resemblance Nominalist is barred from saying this. So what can he say is the foundation for the internal relation?

He cannot desert the nature and say that the foundation is just the individual particulars or tokens, taken as mere particulars and tokens. That would be such a weak foundation for the relation that it would make it possible for anything to resemble anything. That is, resemblance would have to be what it is not: an external relation.

What the Resemblance Nominalist must say, I think, and what is to his advantage to say is that resemblances do flow from the natures of the resembling things, but that these natures are not universal but particular. *a* has a certain nature, *b* has a certain nature. The natures are particular but are such that *a* and *b* must resemble to a certain degree. Given this nature, they resemble to this degree in every possible world in which they are both found.

Here is a way to understand the notion of a particularized nature. We have already seen in Chapter 1 that there are two views on properties: the first, that they are universals; the second, that they are particulars. Let us start, then, by taking properties as particulars. Now take all the properties a thing has and form one big conjunctive but still particular property out of them: P & Q & R & S &. . . . This conjunctive property is on the way to being a particular nature.

But it has not quite got there yet. Resemblance Nominalism, or at any rate the form of Resemblance Nominalism that we are dealing with here, is a blob theory. It does not allow that a thing has many properties, except as a common but potentially misleading manner of speaking for which the theory will try to give satisfactory truth conditions. So now we have, as it were, to congeal the particular properties into a single grand (but still particular) property within which no differentiation can be made. Then we have the particularized nature of a thing. It is these particularized natures to which, I think, the Resemblance Nominalist ought to appeal as the grounding for the internal relation of resemblance.

Should the Resemblance Nominalist then distinguish between a particular and its particularized nature and think of the particular as *having* the nature? That would import some structure, even if a minimal amount, into the blob. It would seem to be more in the spirit of the theory because it would be more economical not to distinguish the particular from the particularized nature. The thing *is* its particularized nature.

But there may be difficulties in the second position. We want to say that a thing might have had at least some different properties from the ones it actually has. The ball is white, but it might have been green. Translated into the language of particularized natures this becomes: The ball's particularized nature might have been other than it is. But if the ball's particularized nature just *is* the ball, then to say that the nature might have been other than it is, is to say that the ball might not have been the ball. So the ball could not have been green.

I suspect, then, that a Resemblance Nominalist who embraces particularized natures will have to distinguish the thing from its nature. But this may not be too high a price to pay for some real advantages. I will now try to show that the doctrine of the particularized nature is of real value to the Resemblance Nominalist. It not only provides him with a foundation for resemblances but enables him to evade important traditional objections to Resemblance Nominalism.

One such objection is this: The theory analyzes what it is to be a token of a certain type in terms of that token's resemblances to other tokens. But what happens if the token lacks any other token to resemble? That is a possible situation. Would the token then not be of that type? Surely not. The type seems to be prior to any resemblance relation the token may have to any other tokens. But is not this just what a *Resemblance* theory is forced to deny? (I myself used this argument against Resemblance Nominalism in the past. See Armstrong 1978a, Ch. 5, Sec. V.)

The doctrine of a particularized nature seems to meet this difficulty. The object has its nature, even if it resembles nothing else. This nature is the foundation for attributing a type to it. There might have been other things with particularized natures, which if they had existed, would have sufficiently resembled the solitary object, but it does not matter that the other things do not exist.

There is another objection to Resemblance Nominalism: Might there not be two nonoverlapping classes of tokens of two different types (the red things and the green things perhaps) that nevertheless have the very same resemblance structure? If we drew up a resemblance map for either class, specifying the precise degree of resemblance each member had to each other, it could be transferred exactly to the other class. But by hypothesis the two classes are classes of things of a different sort or type. How is this possible if type is constituted by resemblance relations? It may be suggested that the things in the two different classes would have different resemblance relations to other things, to third parties outside the two classes. But the reply to this is that the existence of third parties is contingent. The red things would be of the specific type red, and the green things would be of the specific type green, even if everything there is were either red or green.

Particularized natures provide a good answer here also. There seems no reason why two sets of things with particularized natures should not have the same resemblance structure within each of the sets, yet be classes of different sorts of things. So particularized natures are both required (to ground the internal relation of resemblance) and useful (to answer some traditional objections).

## III. Constructing a Resemblance Class

We have not yet considered how a resemblance class can actually be constructed. H. H. Price (1953, Ch. 1, pp. 20–22) does it in this way. We begin with "a small group of standard objects or exemplars." For red objects the members of the group might be "a certain tomato, a certain brick and a certain British post-box." It is allowed, however, that the class as a whole may contain a number of different groups, each of them fitted to be groups of standard objects. What each member of such a group does is to set up a resemblance test. To be red a thing must pass all the tests. A thing passes all the tests by resembling each of the paradigm objects at least as closely as the paradigm objects resemble each other. (To see that there must be a resemblance to each paradigm object, think of a blue brick. It may resemble the red brick paradigm object very closely. But, we would say, the resemblance is in "irrelevant respects." The blue brick is eliminated because it does not have sufficient resemblance to the other members of the standard group.)

The class of colored things is a wider class than the class of red things. For it, the paradigm objects will have to be "set wider apart," that is, the degree of resemblance between them will have to be less. Notice what a heavy weight has to be put upon degrees of resemblance. If the classes are to be objectively there, then the degrees of resemblance will have to be objectively there.

Price sees an advantage here over a Universals theory. On the latter theory the different members of the class will all instantiate the very same universal. Nor can we make much sense of degrees of instantiation. But resemblance admits of degrees, thus allowing for loosely held together classes, involving different degrees of resemblance and with uncertain boundaries. That is just what is needed.

## IV. Identity Conditions for Classes Are No Problem

We saw that because a class is determined by its members, the Natural Class view is in trouble when we consider the possibility of the class's having a different membership. Being an electron would necessarily change if the class of electrons were any bigger or smaller. But this consequence seems absurd.

It is interesting to notice that this difficulty is not a difficulty for the Resemblance theory. Provided that an appropriate resemblance structure is preserved, it does not matter that the class has members added or subtracted. For instance, if H. H. Price's account is correct, all that matters is that there should be at least one paradigm group to set the boundaries, and that a thing have the right resemblance relations to that group, for the thing to be of the type marked out by the paradigms.

Indeed, in an important sense Resemblance Nominalism is not a *class* theory at all. Rather, to be a token of a certain type is to be a term in a suitable resemblance structure of tokens, where the resemblance structure flows from the natures (particular natures) of the tokens. (We shall see, however, that when we come to discuss resemblances involving relations, classes may have to be reintroduced.)

## V. Does Resemblance Determine Type?

We brought the following criticism against the Natural Class theory: It is plausible to say that a token is of a certain type because of the token's nature rather than that a token is of that type because of the class it is a member of. Can we not bring the same sort of difficulty against a Resemblance theory? Do not things resemble each other, to the extent that they do, because of what they are in themselves, in their own nature, rather than that they are of that nature because they resemble? The difficulty already considered in Section II, that a thing may be of a type without anything to resemble, is a close relative of this objection.

If you think of the things, the tokens, as *mere* tokens, simply numerically different from each other, you would have to say that resemblances come first and determine nature. But the doctrine of particularized natures foils this unwelcome conclusion. Once such natures are accepted, the Resemblance Nominalist can say the comfortable thing: that resemblance flows from nature and not nature from resemblance.

It remains true, however, that the particularized natures are a somewhat blunt instrument. Consider the top traffic light at an intersection. It will resemble other red things and other round things. Both these resemblances have to flow from the *one* particularized nature. Yet it is rather natural to distinguish the redness of the light from its roundness and explain these two dimensions of resemblance by reference to two properties. The trouble is that the Resemblance theory, even when filled out with particularized natures, is a blob theory. It does not admit properties. So it cannot make the natural distinction.

## VI. The Causal Argument

The same problem becomes still more pressing if causality is brought into consideration. Go back to the causal argument against the Natural Class theory. We said that a thing acts in virtue of the type of thing it is, yet one wants to say that it is just *the thing* that acts. The other members of the class associated with that type are causally irrelevant. A Resemblance Nominalism can attribute the causal power of a thing to its particularized nature, thus beginning to escape this difficulty.

But trouble remains. We think that things act in virtue of their properties. The object acts on the scalepan in virtue of its mass, and not in virtue of its electric charge. For the Resemblance Nominalist, however, mass and charge are lost inside the single seamless particularized nature. As a result, no complete answer to the causal argument can be given. All that can be said is that the object acts qua resembler of certain things (mass things), rather than qua resembler of other things (charged things). But this reintroduces the causally irrelevant. (It would be troublesome if there were no other massy things and no other charged things.)

## VII. The Coextension Problem Again

We saw that the Natural Class theory, like any class theory, is in difficulty if there can be two different properties that are had by the very same individuals. There is no way of distinguishing the two properties.

The Resemblance theory runs into the same sort of trouble. Suppose that properties P and Q are coextensive. In virtue of this, members of the class of Ps and Qs will have a certain mutual resemblance each to each. But how is the theory to distinguish between the contribution P makes to these resemblances and the contribution made by Q? After all, between any two members of the class there is just a *single* resemblance to a certain degree. The information that the resemblance of the tokens is given by *two* properties is lost inside the single resemblance. There seems no way to recover it. Yet are not coextensive properties at least possible?

## VIII. Relations

There has been little discussion of relations by Resemblance Nominalists. The chief problem seems to be to identify the terms between which the relevant resemblances are supposed to hold. It is a little tricky. Suppose that *a* precedes *b* in time and so does *c* precede *d*. Here we have two states of affairs, and it is natural enough to say that they resemble each other. But Resemblance Nominalism knows nothing about such states of affairs. If there are such entities, then they involve properties and relations—entities that the Resemblance theory is trying to provide a substitute for via resemblance structures.

Does the resemblance hold between the thing composed of the two parts *a* and *b* and the thing composed of the two parts *c* and *d*? The trouble with this answer is that the resemblance we are interested in is not any old resemblance between the two things. One part of the first thing stands to the remainder of the first thing in a way that resembles the way one part of the second thing stands to the remainder of the second thing. But that description already involves the notion of a relation. How is the Resemblance theory to point us in the right direction when it is merely working with resembling things?

Could we solve the problem by allowing the resemblance relation to take a different number of terms in different cases? Where properties such as redness are involved, the relation is two-termed: *Res* (*a*, *b*). But where we have a resemblance between *a*'s preceding *b* and *c*'s preceding *d*, the resemblance would be four-termed: *Res* (*a*, *b*, *c*, *d*). Where the relations to be analyzed involved more than two terms, then the resemblance would link a still greater number of terms. Because of its variable number of terms, resemblance would be what logicians call a multigrade or anadic relation. (Being surrounded by is a typical multigrade relation.)

I do not think that this is satisfactory. It is surely obvious that in the case of the alleged four-termed relation there is a key division after the term *b*. The *a b* complex stands in some way to the *c d* complex. What way? It can only be resemblance. But that is two-term resemblance. We are then back to trying to say what we mean by the *a b* complex and the *c d* complex without bringing in the relation of preceding and which thing precedes which.

It seems, then, that we will have to look to *classes*. The resemblance, we might say, holds between the ordered pair <*a,b*> and <*c, d*>, or else their unordered Wiener-Kuratowski substitutes, {{*a*}, {*a, b*}} and {{*c*}, {*c, d*}}.

But this solution faces the same difficulty that was brought against the Natural Class theory. If the relation involved is asymmetrical or nonsymmetrical then <*a, b*> and <*c, d*> will serve either as *a* succeeds *b* and *c* succeeds *d* or the other way round: *b* succeeds *a* and *d* succeeds *c*. This suggests that the classes *represent* the resemblances but do not constitute them. So we are left with the problem of the true nature of the terms of the resemblance relations. And in any case to appeal to classes means that those difficulties that the Natural Class theory faces that depend on the identity conditions for classes, and that it seemed that Resemblance Nominalism can ignore, cannot be ignored for the case of relations.


## IX. Higher-Order Types

The Resemblance theory faces the same sort of difficulties with higher-order types that the Natural Class theory does. The reason is the same: the absence of properties and relations.

We have already seen that the statements 'red is a color' and 'red resembles orange more than it resembles yellow' cannot be reduced to statements about individual red, orange, and yellow objects. (The same would go for 'a yard is a length' or statements that order the different lengths, such as 'a yard is less than a meter and greater than a foot'.) One might try to analyze 'red is a color' as placing the resemblance class of red things in a certain class of resemblance classes (the color class). Each member of the class of classes (the color class) would resemble each other, in different degrees. But what can be done with 'red resembles orange more than it resembles yellow'? The trouble, we intuit, is that any resemblance between resemblance classes might be determined in its degree of resemblance more by other irrelevant properties of the red, orange, and yellow things, thus swamping the degrees of resemblance bestowed on the objects by their colors.

## X. The Resemblance Regress

We now come to the most famous of all the criticisms of Resemblance Nominalism. The argument was anticipated by J. S. Mill and then formulated more penetratingly by Husserl (for references see Armstrong 1978a, p. 54 n.). But it was given its classical exposition by Bertrand Russell in *The Problems of Philosophy* (1912, pp. 150–151). Here is what he said:

> If we wish to avoid the universals *whiteness* and *triangularity*, we shall choose some particular patch of white or some particular triangle, and say that anything is white or a triangle if it has the right sort of resemblance to our chosen particular. But then the resemblance required will have to be a universal. Since there are many white things, the resemblance must hold between many pairs of particular white things; and this is the characteristic of a universal. It will be useless to say that there is a different resemblance to each pair, for then we will have to say that these resemblances resemble each other, and thus at last we shall be forced to admit resemblance as a universal. The relation of resemblance therefore, must be a true universal and having been forced to admit this universal, we find that it is no

longer worthwhile to invent difficult and implausible theories to avoid the admission of such universals as whiteness and triangularity.

This brilliant argument is an example of what I called a relation regress (perhaps it should be called the fundamental relation regress argument or the nexus regress). The general form of the argument is this. You take the "fundamental relation" used by a particular solution to the Problem of Universals. For Predicate Nominalism this will be *applying to* (as general words apply to objects); for Class Nominalism it will be *class membership*; for Resemblance Nominalism, *resemblance*; for Realism about universals, *instantiation* (a thing's being an instance of a universal). You then ask how the theory is going to deal with its own fundamental relation. As Russell argued in the particular case of resemblance, the procedure leads to a regress because the fundamental relation has to be used again: applied to tokens of itself. But having been used again, it has to be analyzed again, and so ad infinitum. Of course, a regress is not necessarily fatal, because some regresses are virtuous not vicious. (An example of a virtuous regress is the truth regress: $p$, $p$ is true, it is true that $p$ is true, . . . It is quite harmless.) But Russell is in effect arguing that the resemblance regress is vicious because the problem to be solved, namely the question what it is for a token to be of a certain type, turns up again in the alleged solution. The solution uses tokens of the resemblance relation without explaining how the type *resemblance* is brought inside the theory.

Is the argument sound? It is certainly very plausible, and has convinced many people. I used to be convinced by it myself (1978a, Ch. 5, Sec. VI), but now I am not. One major trouble that Russell, and I following him, overlooked is that *all* solutions to the Problem of Universals, including realism about universals, require a fundamental relation. But if so, the regress that Russell finds in the case of resemblance reappears with the other theories. Class membership is a relation. Must not a Class Nominalist analyze the holding of the relation in the same way that he analyzes the holding of other relations? But that was done in terms of ordered classes. For $a$ to precede $b$ is for the ordered class $<a, b>$ to be a member of a certain class of ordered classes: $<a, b> \in \{<a, b>, <c, d>, \ldots \}$. The same type of infinite regress that Russell noticed for resemblance looms. The same thing happens with instantiation. A particular, $a$, instantiates universal F. But what of the relation of instantiation? Must not the pair, $a$ and F, *instantiate* the universal of instantiation, and so ad infinitum?

Russell claims that the resemblance regress is vicious. But if it is vicious in this case, it is hard to deny that it is vicious in all the other cases. They do not seem any different. However, unless you think that the Problem of Universals is a pseudo-problem, and therefore cannot have a solution, that is an impossible conclusion to accept. If, alternatively, it is not vicious in one of the cases, say in the case of the nexus of instantiation, then it will be hard to claim that it is vicious in the case of the other regresses.

Ironically, I now think that the Universals theory is in somewhat more trouble with the relation of instantiation than the Resemblance theory is with the relation of resemblance. That will be discussed in Chapter 5.

Now to say why I think that Russell's argument fails. We have already noted in Section II of this chapter that resemblance is an internal relation, logically dependent upon the terms between which the relation holds. But because the Resemblance theory is a Nominalist theory, that from which the relation flows cannot be the possession of common properties by the related objects. Rather, we said, resemblance must flow internally from the *particularized nature* of the resembling objects.

Given the natures of $a$ and $b$, they must resemble to the exact degree that they do resemble. (Although it would be possible for them to resemble to that exact degree yet have different natures.) The conclusion that I wish to draw from this is that the resemblance is not an additional fact about the world over and above the possession by *a* and *b* of the particularized natures that they have. The relation *supervenes* on the natures, and if it supervenes, I suggest, it is not distinct from what it supervenes upon.

(The notion of supervenience has been much used in contemporary philosophy. Different philosophers have defined it a little differently. I favor, and will use, a definition in terms of possible worlds. Entity Q supervenes on entity P if and only if every possible world that contains P contains Q. This definition allows particular cases of supervenience to be symmetrical: P and Q can supervene on each other. I should add that I think that possible worlds are no more than useful fictions. I work this approach out in a book on the nature of possibility, Armstrong 1989.)

For the case of Resemblance Nominalism the fundamental tie supervenes. I think that this means that we do not have to take it too seriously metaphysically. It is an ontological free lunch. The truth-maker, the ontological ground, that in the world which makes it true that the tie holds, is simply the resembling things. More precisely, according to what I have argued is the best version of the Resemblance theory, the ontological ground is the particularized nature of these things. The tie is not something extra. But if it is not something extra, we do not have to worry abut whether these ties are universals or mere particulars that each resemble each other. The regress is as harmless as, say, the truth regress.

So I think that the Resemblance Nominalist can face down this famous argument. Moreover, and very important, if this suggested reply is correct, then it is also available to a Natural Class Nominalist. *a*'s having the property F is analyzed as *a*'s being a member of the natural class $(a, b, c, \ldots)$. But given the object *a*, and given a certain natural class one of whose members happens to be *a*, the class membership relation supervenes. But if it supervenes, it is not something ontologically additional to the individuals and the natural classes of the individuals. As a result, the regress is as harmless as the truth regress. So I think that both Resemblance Nominalism and the Natural Class theory can evade the nexus regress.

## XI. The Apparatus of the Resemblance Theory

We have seen that provided that we are prepared to postulate particularized natures, then we do not in addition require a resemblance relation. For the resemblances flow from the natures. The resemblance relation has various properties. It admits of degrees, although exact degrees cannot always be assigned very precisely. The scale has an upper limit, exact resemblance, and a lower limit, no resemblance at all. (It is a question whether these limits are ever in fact reached.) Resemblance to a certain degree is always symmetrical, but it is not transitive except for the special case of exact resemblance. If $a$ and $b$ resemble to a certain degree, this degree is unaffected if an object that exactly resembles $a$ is substituted for $a$. The same holds for $b$.

Even although resemblance relations supervene on particularized natures, I think these features of resemblance are part of the ontological cost of the theory. For these features have to be taken as primitive, and therefore unexplained, axioms of resemblance. Particularized natures are such that they necessarily sustain resemblance relations obeying these axioms. A certain theoretical burden, therefore, is placed on the particularized natures. Just how great this theoretical burden is I will bring out later when discussing universals (Chapter 5, Section X). It emerges that once universals are accepted, the formal properties of resemblance can be explained by nothing more mysterious than the formal properties of strict identity.

What of the particularized natures? Do they represent a diseconomy? In some ways they may be an economy. This would be so particularly if we did not need to distinguish between things—tokens—and their natures. If the thing just is the particularized nature, then the thing is being given a minimum of structure. And even if a thing and its nature must be distinguished in some way, as I earlier suggested may be the case, it may still be said to be a more economical scheme than a thing with a whole bunch of separate properties and relations to other things.

At the same time, however, it is likely that this blobbiness of things—this absence of structure in things—is a false economy. For we have seen that, like the Natural Class theory, the resemblance attempt to get along without properties and relations in its fundamental ontological catalogue leads to a great many very difficult problems. The theories now to be investigated, the layer-cake theories, solve this problem at a stroke by allowing the real existence of properties and relations, in greater or lesser numbers. Of course, it may turn out that the new theories push down this conspicuous bulge in the carpet only to have it reappear elsewhere in the carpet, and as bulgy as ever. We will have to see.

# CHAPTER FOUR

# Particulars as Bundles of Universals

## I. Substance-Attribute Versus Bundle Theories

We are now going to allow that there are such things in the world as properties and relations, such things as the mass and charge of electrons, or the betweenness that holds between an amber traffic light, on the one hand, and its red and green companions, on the other. We have not yet decided whether these properties and relations should be taken to be repeatables (universals) or nonrepeatables (particulars, that is, tropes).

One question that immediately comes up is how we ought to understand the relation between an individual thing—a token—and the properties that the thing has. And here we find that two different models compete for the allegiance of philosophers. First, there are Substance-attribute theories and second, there are Bundle theories.

The classical, or standard, theory is the **Substance-attribute**

It is suggested that Part IV, Chapter 8, of Bertrand Russell's *Human Knowledge, Its Scope and Limits* be used as a companion reading to this chapter.

**theory:** It is natural to distinguish a thing, an individual, a token, from any particular properties that the thing happens to have. The table is hard, brown, rectangular, and so on. But it is not identical with its hardness, brownness, rectangularity. These properties are rather naturally taken to be things it merely *has*. (As we have seen, hard-line nominalists do not allow that the thing has any properties, except in a mere manner of speaking.) With thing and properties thus distinguished, even if very intimately connected, we have what may be called a substance-attribute view.

There can be epistemological problems associated with a substance-attribute view. Notoriously these were raised by John Locke. He spoke of the factor of particularity in things, as opposed to their properties, as their substance, or substratum. (As Keith Campbell has suggested to me, the substratum is the nut at the center of the layer cake!)

Before considering Locke's epistemology of substance, let us take note of an important matter of terminology. In the British Empiricist tradition, 'substance' has usually meant the factor of particularity, what Locke called the substratum. The great hostility to substance that you find in the British tradition has been hostility to substratum. Let us call the substratum substance in the thin sense, or the **thin particular**. But now notice that substance can also mean substratum *plus* properties. This is a usage that we associate with Aristotle and the Scholastic philosophers. Let us call this substance in the thick sense. Substratum plus properties constitutes the **thick particular**. Aristotle's primary substances—individual things, this man, this horse—are thick particulars.

Come back now to Locke. For him the substratum, the factor of particularity, the thin particular, is a mere postulate, even if it is one he said that the mind has to make. He called it "something I know not what" that in some mysterious way supports the properties of things. It was this rather unsatisfactory doctrine that led to the British Empiricist suspicion of substance. They were really reacting against Locke's unknowable substratum. This in turn created a climate of opinion favorable to the Bundle theory, which gets rid of substratum by identifying a thing with the bundle of its properties.

But it is not really necessary for a Substance-attribute theorist to take a Lockean line. Why should not such a theorist say that what we actually experience are particulars-having-certain-properties? That seems a good epistemology for the substance-attribute ontology. The particularity of particulars, their having certain properties (and their standing in relations to other particulars) will all be given in our experience of the world. Specifically, all this will be given in our perception of the world.

Before going on, I will call attention to an interesting way that a substance-attribute view might be developed, although I cannot discuss this development at length. Once Locke's view is rejected and substratum is brought into our actual experience of the world, we can begin to wonder just what in experience substratum is to be identified with. An important candidate is the place that a thing is said to occupy or, perhaps even better, the place and time that it occupies. Properties, according to this suggestion, including maybe spatial and temporal properties (shape, size, duration), are supported by, inhere in, or qualify places or place-times.

In support of this suggestion it may be noted that if things occupy different places at the same time, then they must be different things. What if things occupy the same place at different times? The case contemplated can be what ordinary language would describe as the same thing at the two different times—*you* are back here where you started from. However, it is quite plausible to say that in such a case it is different temporal parts of you that are in the same place, so that, strictly, nothing is at the same place at different times.

What would really strengthen the identification of substratum with place-time would be if it were impossible for two different things to be at the very same place *and* time. And it is true that this is what we ordinarily assume. However, there are reasons to think that such a piling up of different things in strictly the same place at the same time may be a possibility. If so, place-time is not the whole story about the particularity of particulars.

Leaving aside this interesting question, we note that in the substance-attribute view the fundamental tie or nexus holding between thin particular and properties appears to be *asymmetrical*. This electron has a certain charge. It is not the case that the charge has the electron.

Contrast this with the fundamental tie in the case of the **bundle** view, where the particular is thought of as a mere bundle of properties. The particular stands to one of its properties as a whole stands to a mere part, and that is asymmetrical. But the really fundamental tie seems to be that between two properties of the same thing, what Russell called *compresence*. That relation is symmetrical.

The substance-attribute view has to be extended to cover relations. (We have already noted that our philosophical tradition tended to play down relations until quite recently—until the twentieth century.) If event *a* precedes event *b*, it is not plausible to see this as a matter of a single thing's having a certain property. We have a different sort of tie or nexus that links together *a*, the relation of preceding, and *b*. The events *a* and *b* have or stand in a certain relation.

It is interesting to notice that the Bundle theory also has to change gear when it comes to relations. If *a* precedes *b*, then you cannot just make a bundle out of *a*'s properties, *b*'s properties, and the relation precedes. Could you perhaps use bundles of bundles, where the lower-level bundles are the *a* bundle, the *b* bundle, with the relation of preceding in a third little bundle of its own? This might possibly work for symmetrical relations, but with an asymmetrical relation it would fail to distinguish *a*'s preceding *b* from *b*'s preceding *a*. These two situations would come out as the very same bundle of bundles.

It looks as if bundling fails here. You just have to relate the bundles, just as a substance-attribute view relates two or more substances. Two or more bundles have or stand in a certain relation.

Therefore, we have a choice of a substance-attribute ontology, plus relations between substances; or a bundle view, plus relations between bundles. But all this time we have been keeping quiet about the nature of properties and relations. Should we take them to be repeatables, that is, to be universals? Or should we take them to be nonrepeatables, to be particulars, to be tropes? Both positions have their attractions.

At once, we get a two-by-two division of theories. We have Substance-attribute theories with universals or with tropes. We have Bundle theories with universals or with tropes:

|  | Universals | Tropes |
|---|---|---|
| Substance-attribute | Traditional    I | Locke    IV<br>C. B. Martin |
| Bundle | Russell    II | G. F. Stout    III<br>D. C. Williams |

All the four boxes are filled. I is the traditional view taken by those who accept universals. II, the bundle-of-universals view, was held by Russell and also by the American philosopher, Brand Blanshard. III, the bundle-of-tropes view, is the orthodox position for a contemporary upholder of tropes. G. F. Stout held it, and D. C. Williams after him. It is currently held by Keith Campbell. It is often not realized that IV, a substance-attribute view with tropes, is a possible view. But I think that it was held, or should have been held, by Locke. I think indeed it is a stronger view than the orthodox trope view held by Stout and Williams. (See Russell 1940, Chs. 6, 8, 24; 1948, Pt. 4, Ch. 8; 1959, Ch. 14; Blanshard 1939, Vol. 1, Chs. 16, 17; 1962, Ch. 9; Stout 1921; 1936; Williams 1966, Ch. 7; Campbell 1981.)

Locke definitely held a substance-attribute view of particulars. As we have just seen, he held it in a rather unlovely form, taking substance (substratum, the thin particular) as the unknowable support of things. But that scepticism-inducing version is not of special interest for us at the moment. Locke was also an explicit nominalist, holding that everything there is, is purely particular. There were no universals in his world. But, finally, he was always talking about the qualities of things. These are properties and he seems to have taken them ontologically seriously. So his qualities ought to be tropes. Yet he did not bundle his properties, rather he had a substance-attribute view.

A contemporary philosopher who accepts a Lockean view is C. B. Martin. In his "Substance Substantiated" (1980) he accepts a substance-attribute view of objects. He explicitly rejects the idea that a particular is a bundle of its properties but takes properties to be particulars, not universals. He attributes the same view to Locke. (Martin does not make substratum unknowable.) See also Denkel, 1989.

We will now consider the interesting, but difficult and not widely held, view that particulars are bundles of universals. It is the most anti-Nominalist view of all. But perhaps it is the least plausible of the four views to be found in our 2 x 2 matrix.

## II. The Identity of Indiscernibles

If the bundle-of-universals view is correct, then it follows that two different things cannot have exactly the same properties, where properties are universals. For given this theory, they would be exactly the same thing. However, against the Bundle theory, it seems possible that two things should have exactly the same properties, that is, be exactly alike. (It is to be noted that, for reasons mentioned in the previous section, positions in space and time do not count as differences in properties. Neither, of course, do such pseudo-properties as being identical with *a*.)

What I have just said is recognized to be an important argument against the bundle-of-universals analysis. (It would have no force against a bundle-of-tropes view.) But to assess the force of the argument we need some preliminaries. First, we must distinguish between nonrelational or intrinsic properties, on the one hand, and relational properties on the other. Relational properties are not to be confused with relations. They involve, but are not the same thing as, relations. An example of a relational property is being 2 centimeters from an electron. It involves the relation type being 2 centimeters from, which is a dyadic relation. But being 2 centimeters from an electron is monadic: It is a property of certain individual things. Notice that properties like being 2 centimeters from *this* electron or living in Australia are also sometimes spoken of as relational properties. But here we will call them impure (as opposed to pure) relational properties because they involve certain particulars: this electron, the continent of Australia. If we are trying to construct particulars out of universals we shall, of course, only be interested in *pure* relational properties.

Having now introduced the notion of a relational property, we turn our attention to two principles that we have already encountered in Chapter 1: the Indiscernibility of Identicals and the Identity of Indiscernibles. The first of these, the **Indiscernibility of Identicals**, says that if *a* is identical with *b*—the morning star with the evening star, Jack the Ripper with Miss X, and so on—then they have all their properties in common. This is a very plausible doctrine and few philosophers think that it is false. It appears that the principle, which may be rendered symbolically as:

$$(\forall x)(\forall y)((x = y) \supset (\forall P)(Px \equiv Py))$$

(for all objects $x$ and $y$, if $x$ is identical with $y$, then $x$ has a property if and only if $y$ has that property) is not only true, but necessarily true. Same thing, same properties.

But the **Identity of Indiscernibles** (which is our present concern) is much more controversial. It is the *converse* of the Indiscernibility of Identicals, and the converse of a truth is not automatically true. It says that if two things have the very same properties, then they are the very same thing. In symbols:

$$(\forall x)(\forall y)((\forall P)(Px \equiv Py) \supset (x = y)).$$

(For all objects $x$ and $y$, if $x$ has a property if and only if $y$ has that property, then $x$ is identical with $y$.)

McTaggart rather helpfully called the Identity of Indiscernibles the "Dissimilarity of the Diverse" (1921, Sec. XCIX). (In logician's terms he took the logically equivalent contrapositive of the above formula.) McTaggart's formulation brings out very clearly that if particulars are just bundles of universals, then different particulars must contain at least one different universal.

We may now distinguish between a strong and a weak form of the Identity of Indiscernibles. In the *strong* form we confine ourselves to nonrelational properties. To satisfy the strong form of the Identity of Indiscernibles as applied to the Bundle theory, any two particulars must have at least one different nonrelational property. The *weak* form of the principle lets in relational properties. Any two particulars must have at least one different property, but it could be a mere relational property.

Let us consider in turn these two possibilities for the Bundle theory. Suppose first that it turns out to be necessary for a Bundle theorist to uphold the strong version of the theory. Is it defensible? The strong version does not seem to be a necessary truth. Surely it is possible that two numerically different things could have *exactly* the same nonrelational properties? It might still be wondered whether the strong view is not true as a matter of contingent fact. There is a famous passage from Leibniz:

> There is no such thing as two individuals indiscernible from each other. An ingenious gentleman of my acquaintance, discoursing with me, in the presence of her Electoral Highness the Princess Sophia, in the garden of Herrenhausen; thought he could find two leaves perfectly alike. The Princess defied him to do it, and he ran all over the garden a long time to look for some; but it was to no purpose. Two drops of water, or milk, viewed with a microscope, will appear distinguishable from each other. (p. 36 in the H. G. Alexander edition of *The Leibniz-Clarke Correspondence*)

But what about the submicroscopic level? It would seem that two electrons, for instance, could have exactly the same nonrelational properties. It appears to be physically possible. Perhaps from time to time the possibility is actualized.

In any case, however, could a Bundle theorist hold that the identity of a thing with the bundle of its nonrelational properties is contingent only? This is not a very plausible position (and not one held by Leibniz). It would seem that if the Bundle theory is true, it is a theory about the essential constitution of individual things, namely, that they are bundles of properties. That would make the theory a necessary truth, if it is true at all. And then to falsify it, all that is needed is the mere logical possibility of two things with exactly the same nonrelational properties. That logical possibility seems to obtain.

The moral of all this is that the Bundle theorist is in serious difficulties if he holds the strong view. If we suppose that he takes the weak view and identifies a thing with the bundle of its nonrelational plus relational properties, do things improve? Then a difference in relational properties will be enough, although these relational properties must be universals.

The matter is a bit more controversial, but even in its weak version the Identity of Indiscernibles does not appear to be a necessary truth. Various cases have been thought up to try to support this conclusion. One interesting case is the possibility of eternal return. Suppose that the history of the universe is cyclical, with no first cycle and the cycles repeating themselves exactly, down to the smallest detail, and doing so forever. It can be seen that an object in one cycle and its counterparts in all the other cycles are not merely internally exactly the same but that their relational properties are exactly the same, including relations to previous and succeeding cycles. Remember that the relational properties must be pure (wholly universal). Note also that if there were a first or a last cycle, then you could differentiate cycles, and the things in them, by different relational properties (seventeenth cycle from nothing).

This case can be challenged. You can argue that what you get at the end of a cycle is not a new token of exactly the same type as that at the beginning of the cycle, but rather the very same token. You can argue, that is, that the case given is really one where time is circular and that any event is both before and after itself. Then the case would not be a counterinstance to the thesis that the weak Identity of Indiscernibles is a necessary truth.

In reply to this, though it may be a logical possibility that time is circular in this way (compare finite but unbounded space), it does not seem that we have to redescribe the case in this way. Infinite repetition, where the cycles are type-identical, yet are different tokens, seems also to be a possibility. If so, the weak Identity of Indiscernibles is only a contingent truth. (It is hard to believe that it is actually false.)

Robert Adams (1979) has discovered a very beautiful argument for the possibility of the exact repetition of numerically identical cycles. It may be called "the argument from almost indiscernible cycles." It can hardly be denied that it is possible that the universe is infinite in time, infinite at both ends. Suppose that it goes in cycles, say, expansion followed by contraction, and that the cycles are more or less the same. This surely is a possibility. Now make the cycles more and more alike. Get them so that the different cycles differ only in the exact excitation levels of a few electrons. Again, this should be a possibility. Now why cannot we close the small remaining gap? Why cannot we reach *exact* likeness of each of the cycles while keeping the cycles numerically distinct, keeping them as distinct tokens?

Think of the matter in terms of possibility. For each electron in the different, but closely resembling, series, is it not possible that their levels of excitation, et cetera, should have been a little bit different? These possibilities for each electron are surely logically independent of each other. But if independent, there is one distribution of possibilities that will give strict type identity to each of the infinite repetitions. The argument is not logically conclusive, but it appears very strong.

So even the weak version of the Identity of Indiscernibles appears not to be a necessary truth. To use this version, therefore, the Bundle theorist would have to maintain that it is only contingently true that each particular is a different bundle of universals.

David Lewis has pointed out to me that one could bring a new version of the Adams argument against this contingency position. Start with a possible world involving the eternal repetition of very nearly indiscernible cycles. Suppose also that it is assumed that the Bundle theory is contingently true only. And yet if, in that world, only a few electrons had behaved a little differently, then the cycles would have been exactly the same, the Bundle theory would not have been true, and different particulars would have involved a factor of particularity over and above their properties. Those electrons have an absurd importance! (Notice that this sort of argument could also be brought against a contingency version of the strong Bundle theory.) It seems, then, that the Bundle theory faces serious difficulties both in the strong and the weak version.

## III. Problems of Constructing the Bundle

We have spoken airily of a bundle of universals, but it turns out that there are difficulties in actually constructing the bundle. Russell began with a fundamental, not further analyzable, relation, which he called compresence (1948, p. 312). Intuitively, it is the relation that holds between any two properties that are properties of the same thing. But since Russell was going to use the relation to build up ordinary things, that can be an informal explanation only.

Another intuitive way to think of compresence is being in the same place and time. But notice that the properties that are going to be compresent will have to include spatial and temporal properties: shape, size, and duration. In any case, space and time, being physical entities, are among the things that have to be constructed as bundles of universals.

What are the formal properties of compresence? First, and obviously, it is symmetrical. If property A is compresent with property B, then B is compresent with A. However, it is not transitive. If A is compresent with B, and B with C, then it is not necessary that A is compresent with C. You can see that this will have to be so by considering particular $x$, which has properties A and B but not C, and particular $y$, which has B and C but not A. From $x$ we have Comp (A, B); from $y$ we have Comp (B, C). But we do not have Comp (A, C), which we need for transitivity. Of course, there can be a third particular, which has A and C, thus giving us Comp (A, C). But obviously there need not be such a particular. Perhaps there is not one. For instance, the laws of nature may forbid the compresence of A and C in any particular.

So compresence is a symmetrical and nontransitive relation.

It is nontransitive because the terms of the relation are universals. Suppose that what we were dealing with were tropes: properties as particulars rather than universals. Compresence could then be symmetrical and *transitive* because properties would, as it were, not stray outside the bundle. In general, symmetrical and transitive relations operating upon a domain can mark things off into nice exclusive bundles—into "equivalence classes." But with a symmetrical and nontransitive relation, the job of setting up the bundles may be more difficult. So in fact it proves.

Having introduced the relation of compresence, Russell then defines the notion of a complex of compresence. This is a class of universals, each member of which has the compresence relation to each other member. This is quite a closely knit structure. A model is a mutual admiration society, where every member admires every other member.

This paves the way for the notion of a complete complex of compresence. This is a complex of compresent universals, but one to which no further universals can be added because any such universal would fail to be compresent with at least one member of the group. (You cannot enlarge the mutual admiration society any further.) Russell then says that a particular can be identified as a complete complex of compresence.

This is a clever construction, but alas it does not work. It falls victim to a difficulty pointed out by Nelson Goodman (1966, Ch. 5, Sec. 3) which he called "the difficulty of imperfect community." (In Armstrong 1978a, Ch. 9, Sec. III, I wrongly attributed the difficulty to Michael Tooley, who rediscovered it without realizing that the argument had been anticipated by Goodman.) Suppose that object $a$ has properties P and Q but not R, $b$ has Q and R but not P, while $c$ has P and R but not Q. Suppose also that nothing is P and Q and R. (That last is a law of nature.) Then we have Comp (P, Q), Comp (Q, R), and Comp (P, R). Given Russell's definition, {P, Q, R} form a complex of compresence. Either it is a complete complex, or it is not. If it is complete, then there are complete complexes that do not constitute a single particular. (A complete complex of compresence [CCC] is not *sufficient* to yield a particular.) If it is not complete, add universals until it is complete. Since P, Q, and R cannot be properties of just one thing, still we have a CCC that is spread over more than one particular. Hence CCCs that do not constitute a single particular are definitely possible. Being a complete complex of compresence may perhaps be necessary for being a single particular, but it is by no means sufficient.

A construction that is more complex and artificial than a complete complex of compresence is available and to some extent at least gets round this difficulty. But I will not go further with the matter here. (See Armstrong 1978a, Ch. 9, Sec. IV. There the new construction is again attributed to Tooley. It was actually anticipated by Goodman 1966, Ch. 6, Secs. 4, 5. But as indicated in my 1978a, the new construction still faces difficulties, although of a more rarefied sort than imperfect community.)

## IV. A Further Problem with Compresence

We have seen that a complete complex of compresence is not sufficient to yield a particular. There can be CCCs that are not particulars. But equally it appears that there can be particulars that are not CCCs. Being a complete complex of compresence is not necessary for being a particular.

Consider a particular and let it have a near twin, another particular that exactly resembles the first particular except that the near twin lacks one or more properties that the first particular has. Perhaps the first particular is colored, whereas the near twin is totally transparent. Some might consider lacking all color to be itself a property, but I believe that there are good grounds for denying that absences of properties are themselves properties. With this premiss granted, the argument proceeds.

What we have now, on the Bundle-of-universals theory, is two bundles, one of which is a mere or proper part of the other. But then it is clear that the smaller bundle cannot be a complete complex of comprecent universals. So being a CCC is neither sufficient nor necessary for being a particular.


## V. Can Universals Be the Substance of the World?

Those who try to construct particulars out of universals are proposing that the world is a construction from, is constituted by, universals. We can put this another way by saying that they are proposing that universals are the substance of the world. (Substance here is not substratum, nor is it the thing plus all its properties. It is a third sense of the word 'substance'.)

A definition of substance in this sense of the word, which is accepted by many metaphysicians, is that substance is something that is capable of independent existence. Substances may depend upon other substances, causally for instance, but it will at least be a logical possibility for individual substances to exist in complete independence. A substance logically requires nothing beyond itself for its existence. It could be the only thing in the universe.

If we accept this line of thought about substances (and I am inclined to think that we should), and if universals are the sole substance of the world, then rather radical consequences have to be drawn. One thing that will be possible is for individual universals to exist in independence of any other universals—to exist outside any bundle. You could have a possible world that consisted of a number of universals existing in independence of each other. Using the language of a Substance-attribute theory, we could say that they would form a realm of uninstantiated universals (see Chapter 5, Section I).

But this may be a reductio ad absurdum of the bundle-of-universals theory. If having mass M, or having charge C, where M and C are determinate values, are universals, as it is plausible to suggest, then it seems very strange that such a mass and a charge could exist without being the mass or charge *of* something. The matter seems even stranger when we come to consider relations. Can preceding exist without things to precede and be preceded by? Of course, the bundle theorist might surrender the case of relations and allow that *they* must have terms. But will this not strengthen the case for saying that properties, equally, cannot exist on their own?

When we come to consider tropes, that is, properties and relations taken to be particulars, we will note that trope theorists often hold that tropes are the true substance of the world. That doctrine leads to similar, quite difficult consequences. But a trope is at least a particular. A universal as a substance is a peculiarly repugnant notion.

This concludes our examination of the Bundle-of-universals theory. We have seen the difficulties for this position that flow from the necessity to uphold certain versions of the Identity of Indiscernibles. We have seen difficulties in spelling out the bundling principle that holds together the totality of the properties "of" a particular. (Being a complete complex of compresent universals seems to be neither sufficient nor necessary for being a particular.) Finally, this view makes universals into the substance of the world. But if substance in this sense is allowed its usual prerogative of being capable of independent existence, then it is unclear that universals can be substances. I think that an upholder of universals does better to think of them as *attributes* of particulars. To that classical form for a theory of universals we now turn.

# CHAPTER FIVE

# Universals as Attributes

## I. Uninstantiated Universals?

If we abandon the idea that particulars are nothing but bundles of universals but still want to recognize universals, then we must return to the traditional view that particulars, tokens, *instantiate* universals: having properties and standing to each other in relations. If we do this, then there are a number of controversial questions that have to be settled. One key question is this. Should we, or should we not, accept a **Principle of Instantiation** for universals? That is, should we, or should we not, demand that every universal be instantiated? That is, for each property universal must it be the case that it is a property of some particular? For each relation universal must it be the case that there are particulars between which the relation holds?

We certainly should not demand that every universal should be instantiated *now*. It would be enough if a particular universal was not instantiated now, but was instantiated in the past, or would be instantiated in the future. The Principle of Instantiation should be interpreted as ranging over all time:

It is suggested that Chapter 11 of D. M. Armstrong's *Nominalism and Realism* and Chapters 13–17 of his *A Theory of Universals* be used as companion readings to this chapter.

past, present, and future. But should we uphold the principle even in this relatively liberal form?

This is a big parting of the ways. We can call the view that there are uninstantiated universals the Platonist view. It appears to have been the view held by Plato, who was also, apparently, the first philosopher to introduce universals. (He spoke of Forms or Ideas—but there was nothing psychological about the Ideas.)

Once you have uninstantiated universals you need somewhere special to put them, a "Platonic heaven," as philosophers often say. They are not to be found in the ordinary world of space and time. And since it seems that any instantiated universal might have been uninstantiated—for example, there might have been nothing past, present, or future that had that property—then if uninstantiated universals are in a Platonic heaven, it will be natural to place all universals in that heaven. The result is that we get two realms: the realm of universals and the realm of particulars, the latter being ordinary things in space and time. Such universals are often spoken of as *transcendent*. (A view of this sort was explicitly held by Russell in his earlier days before he adopted a bundle-of-universals view. See his introductory book *The Problems of Philosophy*, 1912, Chs. 9 and 10.) Instantiation then becomes a very big deal: a relation between universals and particulars that crosses realms. The Latin tag used by the Scholastics for a theory of this sort is *universalia ante res*, "universals before things." Such a view is unacceptable to Naturalists, that is, to those who think that the space-time world is all the world that there is. This helps to explain why Empiricists, who tend to be sympathetic to Naturalism, often reject universals.

It is interesting to notice that a separate-realm theory of universals permits of a blob as opposed to a layer-cake view of particulars. For on this view, what is it for a thing to have a property? It is not the thing's having some internal feature, but rather its having a relationship, the instantiation relationship, to certain universals or Forms in another realm. The thing itself could be bloblike. It is true that the thing could also be given a property structure. But then the properties that make up this structure cannot be universals but must be particulars. They would have to be tropes. Perhaps this second possibility is the natural candidate for the sixth box in the diagram in Chapter 1 (Section III). The particular involves property tropes, but these property tropes are put into natural classes by their instantiating a certain universal in the realm of the universals. At any rate, without bringing in tropes in addition it seems that Platonic theories of universals have to treat particulars as bloblike rather than layer-caked. I think that this is an argument against Platonic theories.

If, however, we reject uninstantiated universals, then we are at least in a position, if we want to do it, to bring the universals down to earth. We can adopt the view whose Latin tag is *universalia in rebus*, "universals in things." We can think of a thing's properties as constituents of the thing and think of the properties as universals. This may have been the position of Aristotle. (The scholars differ. Some make him a Nominalist. Some think he believed in this-worldly universals. Certainly, he criticized Plato's otherworldly universals.) *Universalia in rebus* is, of course, a layer-cake view, with properties as universals as part of the internal structure of things. (Relations will be *universalia inter res*, "universals between things" [Abbott 1886].)

There are difficulties in this position, of course, objections that can be brought, as with every other solution to the Problem of Universals. One thing that has worried many philosophers, including perhaps Plato, is that on this view we appear to have multiple location of the same thing. Suppose *a* is F and *b* is also F, with F a property universal. The very same entity has to be part of the structure of two things at two places. How can the universal be in two places at once? I will come back to this question later in this chapter.

Just to round things off I will mention the third Scholastic tag: *universalia post res*, "universals after things." This was applied to Nominalist theories. It fits best with **Predicate** or **Concept Nominalism**, where properties, et cetera, are as it were created by the classifying mind: shadows cast on things by our predicates or concepts.

But our present task is to decide whether or not we ought to countenance uninstantiated universals. The first point to be made is that the onus of proof seems to be firmly on the side of the Platonists. It can hardly be doubted that there is a world of space and time. But a separate realm of universals is a mere hypothesis, or postulation. If a postulation has great explanatory value, then it may be a good postulation. But it has to prove itself. Why should we postulate uninstantiated universals?

One thing that has moved many philosophers is what we may call the argument from the meaning of general terms. Plato, in his *Republic*, had Socrates say, "shall we proceed as usual and begin by assuming the existence of a single essential nature or Form for every set of things which we call by the same name?" (595, trans. F. M. Cornford). Socrates may have been thinking along the following lines. Ordinary names, that is, proper names, have a bearer of the name. If we turn to general terms—words like 'horse' and 'triangular' that apply to many different things—then we need something that stands to the word in the same general sort of relation that the bearer of the proper name stands to the proper name. There has to be an object that constitutes or corresponds to the meaning of the general word. So there has to be something called horseness, and triangularity. But now consider a general word that applies to nothing particular at all, a word like 'unicorn' for instance. It is perfectly meaningful. And if it is meaningful, must there not be something in the world that constitutes or corresponds to the word? So there must be uninstantiated universals.

This "argument from meaning" is a very bad argument. (In fairness to Socrates, it is not clear whether he was using it.

Other philosophers have, though, often at a rather unself-conscious level.) The argument depends on the assumption that in every case where a general word has meaning, there is something in the world that constitutes or corresponds to that meaning. Gilbert Ryle spoke of this as the 'Fido'-Fido fallacy. Fido corresponds to the word 'Fido', but there does not have to be some single thing corresponding to a general word.

To go along with the argument from meaning is to be led into a very promiscuous theory of universals. If it is correct, then we know a priori that for each general word with a certain meaning, there exists a universal. This lines up predicates and properties in a nice neat way, but it is a way that we ought to be very suspicious of. Is it that easy to discover what universals there are?

Plato had another line of thought that led him toward uninstantiated universals. This is the apparent failure of things in the ordinary world to come up to exact standards. It seems that nothing in the world is perfectly straight or circular, yet in geometry we discuss the properties of perfectly straight lines or perfect circles. Again, no thing is perfectly changeless. Yet again, it may well be that no act is perfectly just. Certainly no person is perfectly virtuous and no state is perfectly just. Yet in ethical and political discussion (e.g., in the *Republic*) we can discuss the nature of virtue and justice. In general, we perceive the world as falling short of certain standards. This can be explained if, whether we know it or not, we are comparing ordinary things to Forms, which the ordinary things can never fully instantiate. (This can lead one, and perhaps led Plato, to the difficult notion of degrees of instantiation, with the highest degree never realized.)

It is interesting to notice that this argument did not quite lead Plato where he wanted to go in every case. Consider geometry. In geometry one might wish to consider the properties of, say, two intersecting circles. These circles will be perfectly circular. But also, of course, there is only *one* Form of the circle. So what are these two perfect circles? Plato, apparently, had to introduce what he called the Mathematicals. Like the mathematical Forms they were perfect and thus were unlike ordinary things. But unlike the Forms, there could be many tokens of the same type, and in this they were like ordinary things. They were particulars, although perfect particulars. But if this is so, though perhaps the falling away from standards gave Plato an argument for the Mathematicals, it is not clear that it is any argument for the Forms.

But in any case, cannot ideal standards simply be things that we merely think of? We can quite knowingly form thoughts of that which does not exist. In the case of ideal standards nothing comes up to the standard, but by extrapolating from ordinary things that approximate to the standard in different degrees, we can form the thought of something that does come up to the standard. It turns out to be useful to do so. Why attribute metaphysical reality to such standards? They could be useful fictions. As a matter of fact, in the geometrical case it appears that such notions as that of a perfectly straight line or a perfectly circular object may be acquired directly in experience. For cannot something look perfectly straight or perfectly circular, even if it is not in fact so?

One should note that one thing that seems to keep a theory of uninstantiated universals going is the widespread idea that it is sufficient for a universal to exist if it is merely possible that it should be instantiated. I have found in discussion that this idea has particular appeal if it is empirically possible (that is, compatible with the laws of nature) that the alleged universal should have actual instances. Suppose, for instance, that somebody describes a very complex pattern of wallpaper but does not ever sketch the pattern or manufacture the wallpaper. Suppose nobody else does either in the whole history of the universe. It is clear that there was nothing in the laws of nature that prevented the pattern's ever having an instance, from ever having a token of the type. But is not that pattern a monadic universal, a complex and structural universal to be sure, but a universal nonetheless?

In this way, apparently, it is natural for philosophers to argue. But for myself I do not see the force of the argument. Philosophers do not reason that way about particulars. They do not argue that it is empirically possible that present-day France should be a monarchy and therefore that the present king of France exists, although, unfortunately for French royalists, he is not instantiated. Why argue in the same way about universals? Is it that philosophers think that universals are so special that they can exist whether or not particular things, which are contingent only, exist? If so, I think that this is no better than a prejudice, perhaps inherited from Plato.

There is one subtle variation of the argument to uninstantiated universals from their empirical possibility that I think has more weight. It has been developed by Michael Tooley (1987, 3.1.4 and 3.2). However, it depends upon deep considerations about the nature of the laws of nature, which cannot be discussed here. And in any case, the argument depends upon the laws' being found to have a very special structure, which it is unlikely that they actually have. As a result, it seems that the best that the argument shows is that uninstantiated universals are possible rather than actual. And even this conclusion may be avoidable (see Armstrong 1983, Ch. 8).

It may also be thought that considerations from mathematics, and the properties and relations postulated by mathematicians, push toward the recognition of uninstantiated universals. However, the whole project of bringing together the theory of universals with the disciplines of mathematics, although very important, cannot be undertaken here. I have sketched out, rather broadly, the way that I think it ought to go in a book on the nature of possibility (1989, Chapter 10).

From this point on, therefore, I am going to assume the truth of the Principle of Instantiation. As already noted, this does not compel one to abandon a two-realm doctrine. It does not compel one to bring the universals down among ordinary things. But it does *permit* one to do this, and to do so seems the natural way to develop the theory once one rejects uninstantiated universals.

## II. Disjunctive, Negative, and Conjunctive Universals

For simplicity, in this section I will consider property universals only. But the points to be made appear to apply to relations also. We have already rejected uninstantiated universals. But it seems that the potential class of universals needs to be cut down a great deal further if we are to get a plausible theory. I will begin by giving reasons for rejecting disjunctive property universals. By a **disjunctive property** I mean a disjunction of (property) universals. Let us assume that particular electric charges and particular masses are universals. Then having charge C or having mass M (with C and M dummies for determinate, that is, definite values) would be an example of a disjunctive property. Why is it not a universal? Consider two objects. One has charge C but lacks mass M. The other lacks charge C but has mass M. So they have the disjunctive property having charge C or having mass M. But surely that does not show that, in any serious sense, they thereby have something identical? The whole point of a universal, however, is that it should be identical in its different instances.

There is another reason to deny that a disjunction of universals is a universal. There is some very close link between universals and causality. The link is of this nature. If a thing instantiates a certain universal, then, in virtue of that, it has the power to act in a certain way. For instance, if a thing has a certain mass, then it has the power to act upon the scalepan of a balance, or upon scales, in a certain way. Furthermore, different universals bestow different powers. Charge and mass, for instance, manifest themselves in different ways. I doubt if the link between universals and powers is a necessary one, but it seems real. Moreover, if, as seems abstractly possible, two different universals bestowed the very same powers, how could one ever know that they were two different universals? If they affect all apparatus, including our brains, in exactly the same way, will we not judge that we are dealing with one universal only?

Now suppose that a thing has charge C but lacks mass M. In virtue of charge C, it has certain powers to act. For instance, it repels things with like charge. Possession of the disjunctive property C or M adds nothing to its power. This suggests that while C may be a genuine universal, C or M is not.

So I think that we should reject disjunctive universals. A similar case seems to hold against negative universals: the lack or absence of a property is not a property. If having charge C is the instantiation of a universal, then not having C is not the instantiating of a universal.

First, we may appeal to identity again. Is there really something in common, something identical, in everything that lacks charge C? Of course, there might be some universal property that just happened to be coextensive with lacking charge C. But the lack itself does not seem to be a factor found in each thing that lacks charge C.

Second, causal considerations seem to point in the same direction. It is a strange idea that lacks or absences do any causing. It is natural to say that a thing acts in virtue of positive factors alone. This also suggests that absences of universals are not universals.

It is true that there is some linguistic evidence that might be thought to point the other way. We do say things like 'lack of water caused his death'. At the surface, the statement says that a lack of water caused an absence of life. But how seriously should we take such ways of expressing ourselves? Michael Tooley has pointed out that we are unhappy to say 'lack of poison causes us to remain alive'. Yet if the surface way of understanding the first statement is correct, then the second statement should be understood in the same way and thought to be true. Certain counterfactual statements are true in both cases: If he had had water, then he would (could) have still been alive; if we had taken poison, we would have been dead now. These are causal truths. But they tell us very little about the actual causal factors operative in the two cases. We believe, I think, that these actual causal factors could be spelled out in purely positive terms.

It is interesting to notice that conjunctions of universals (having both charge C and mass M) escape the two criticisms leveled against disjunctive and negative universals. With conjunctions we do have identity. The very same conjunction of factors is present in each instance. There is no problem about causality. If a thing instantiates the conjunction, then it will have certain powers as a consequence. These powers will be different from those that the thing would have had if it had had just one of the conjuncts. It may even be that the conjunction can do more than the sum of what each property would do if each was instantiated alone. (As scientists say: There could be synergism. The effect could be more than the sum of each cause acting by itself.)

But there is one condition that ought to be put on conjunctive universals. Some thing (past, present, future) must actually have both properties and at the same time. This, of course, is simply the Principle of Instantiation applied to conjunctive universals.

### III. Predicates and Universals

What has been said about uninstantiated universals, and also about disjunctions and negations of universals, has brought out a most important point. It is that there is no automatic passage from predicates (linguistic entities) to universals. For instance, the expression 'either having charge C or having mass M' is a perfectly good predicate. It could apply to, or be true of, innumerable objects. But as we have seen, this does not mean that there is a universal corresponding to this predicate.

Wittgenstein made a famous contribution to the Problem of Universals with his discussion of **family resemblances**. Wittgenstein was an antimetaphysician, and his object was to dissolve rather than to solve the Problem of Universals. He seems to have thought that what he said about family resemblances was (among other things) a step toward getting rid of the problem. But I think that the real moral of what he said is only that predicates and universals do not line up in any simple way.

In his *Philosophical Investigations* (1953, Secs. 66 and 67) he considered the notion of a *game*. He had this to say about it:

66. Consider for example the proceedings that we call "games". I mean board-games, card-games, ball-games, Olympic games, and so on. What is common to them all?—Don't say: "There *must* be something common, or they would not be called 'games'"—but *look and see* whether there is anything common to all.—For if you look at them you will not see something that is common to *all*, but similarities, relationships, and a whole series of them at that. To repeat: don't think, but look!—Look for example at board-games, with their multifarious relationships. Now pass to card-games; here you find many correspondences with the first group, but many common features drop out, and others appear. When we pass next to ball-games, much that is common is retained, but much is lost.—Are they all 'amusing'? Compare chess with noughts and crosses. Or is there always winning and losing, or competition between players? Think of patience. In ball games there is winning and losing; but when a child throws his ball at the wall and catches it again, this feature has disappeared. Look at the parts played by skill and luck; and at the games like ring-a-ring-a-roses; here is the element of amusement, but how many other characteristic features have disappeared! And we can go through the many, many other groups of games in the same way; we can see how similarities crop up and disappear.

And the result of this examination is: we see a complicated

network of similarities overlapping and criss-crossing: some—
times overall similarities, sometimes similarities of detail.

67. I can think of no better expression to characterize these
similarities than "family resemblances"; for the various
resemblances between members of a family: build, features,
colour of eyes, gait, temperament, etc. etc. overlap and criss-
cross in the same way.—And I shall say: 'games' form a family.

This has been a very influential passage. Wittgenstein and
his followers applied the point to all sorts of notions besides
those of a game, including many of the central notions discussed
by philosophers. But what should a believer in universals
think that Wittgenstein has shown about universals?

Let us agree, as we probably should, that there is no
universal of gamehood. But now what of this "complicated
network of similarities overlapping and criss-crossing" of
which Wittgenstein speaks? All the Realist has to do is to
analyze each of these similarities in terms of common
properties. That analysis of similarity is not a difficult or
unfamiliar idea, though it is an analysis that would be
contested by a Nominalist. But there will not be any property
that runs through the whole class and makes them all games.
To give a crude and oversimplified sketch, the situation might
be like this:

| Particulars: | *a* | *b* | *c* | *d* | *e* |
|---|---|---|---|---|---|
| Their properties: | FGHJ | GHJK | HJKL | JKLM | KLMN |

Here F to N are supposed to be genuine property universals, and
it is supposed that the predicate "game" applies in virtue of
these properties. But the class of particulars (*a* ... *e*), which is
the class of all tokens of games, is a family in Wittgenstein's
sense. Here, though, I have sketched an account of such
families that is completely compatible with Realism about
universals.

However, Wittgenstein's remarks do raise a big question. How does one decide whether one is or is not in the presence of a genuine property or relation? Wittgenstein says of games, "don't think, but look." As a general recipe, at least, that seems far too simple.

I do not think that there is any infallible way of deciding what are the true universals. It seems clear that we must not look to semantic considerations. As I said in Section I of this chapter, those who argue to particular universals from semantic data, from predicates to a universal corresponding to that predicate, argue in a very optimistic and unempirical manner. I call them a priori realists. Better, I think, is a posteriori realism. The best guide that we have to just what universals there are is total science.

For myself, I believe that this puts physics in a special position. There seem to be reasons, (scientific, empirical, a posteriori reasons) to think that physics is *the* fundamental science. If that is correct, then such properties as mass, charge, extension, duration, space-time interval, and other properties envisaged by physics may be the true monadic universals. (They are mostly ranges of quantities. Quantities raise problems that will need some later discussion.) Spatio-temporal and causal relations will perhaps be the true polyadic universals.

If this is correct, then the ordinary types—the type red, the type horse, in general, the types of the manifest image of the world—will emerge as preliminary, rough-and-ready, classifications of reality. For the most part they are not false, but they are rough-and-ready. Many of them will be family affairs, as games appear to be. To the one type will correspond a whole family of universals and not always a very close family. And even where the ordinary types do carve the beast of reality along its true joints, they may still not expose those joints for the things that they are. But let it be emphasized that any identification of universals remains rather speculative. In what I have just been saying I have been trying to combine a philosophy of universals with Physicalism. Others may have other ideas.


## IV. States of Affairs

In the Universals theory that we are examining, particulars instantiate properties, pairs of particulars instantiate (dyadic) relations, triples of particulars instantiate (triadic) relations, and so on as far as is needed. Suppose that $a$ is F, with F a universal, or that $a$ has R to $b$, with R a universal. It appears that we are required to recognize $a$'s being F and $a$'s having R to $b$ as items in our ontology. I will speak of these items as **states of affairs**. Others have called them facts (e.g., Wittgenstein 1961, Skyrms 1981).

Why do we need to recognize states of affairs? Why not recognize simply particulars, universals (divided into properties and relations), and, perhaps, instantiation? The answer appears by considering the following point. If $a$ is F, then it is entailed that $a$ exists and that the universal F exists. However, $a$ could exist, and F could exist, and yet it fail to be the case that $a$ is F (F is instantiated, but instantiated elsewhere only). $a$'s being F involves something more than $a$ and F. It is no good simply adding the fundamental tie or nexus of instantiation to the sum of $a$ and F. The existence of $a$, of instantiation, and of F does not amount to $a$'s being F. The something more must be $a$'s being F—and this is a state of affairs.

This argument rests upon a general principle, which, following C. B. Martin, I call the truth-maker principle. According to this principle, for every contingent truth at least (and perhaps for all truths contingent or necessary) there must be something in the world that makes it true. "Something" here may be taken as widely as may be wished. The "making" is not causality, of course: Rather, it is that in the world in virtue of which the truth is true. Gustav Bergmann and his followers have spoken of the "ontological ground" of truths, and I think that this is my "something in the world" that makes truths true. An important point to notice is that different truths may all have the same truth-maker, or ontological ground. For instance, that this thing is colored, is red, and is scarlet are all made true by the thing's having a particular shade of color.

The truth-maker principle seems to me to be fairly obvious once attention is drawn to it, but I do not know how to argue for it further. It is to be noted however that some of those who take perfectly seriously the sort of metaphysical investigation that we are here engaged upon nevertheless reject the principle (see in particular Lewis 1986c).

Accepting the truth-maker principle will lead one to reject Quine's view (1961) that *predicates* do not have to be taken seriously in considering the ontological implications of statements one takes to be true. Consider the difference between asserting that a certain surface is red and asserting that it is green. An upholder of the truth-maker principle will think that there has to be an ontological ground, a difference in the world, to account for the difference between the predicate 'red' applying to the surface and the predicate 'green' so applying. Of course, what that ontological ground is, is a further matter. There is no high road from the principle to universals and states of affairs.

Returning now to states of affairs, it may be pointed out that there are some reasons for accepting states of affairs even if the truth-maker principle is rejected. First, we can apparently refer to states of affairs, preparatory to saying something further about them. But it is generally, if not universally, conceded by philosophers that what can be referred to exists. Second, states of affairs are plausible candidates for the terms of causal relations. The state of affairs of $a$'s being F may be the cause of $b$'s being G. Third, as we shall see in Section VIII of this chapter, states of affairs can help to solve a fairly pressing problem in the theory of universals: how to understand the multiple location of property universals and the nonlocation of relation universals.

It is interesting to see that states of affairs seem not to be required by a Class Nominalist or a Resemblance Nominalist, and of course that is an important economy for their respective theories. The Class Nominalist analyzes *a*'s being F as *a*'s being a member of a class (or natural class) containing {*a, b, c, . . .* }. But here we have simply *a* and the class. The class-membership relation is internal, dictated by the nature of the terms. So we need not recognize it as something additional to the terms. The terms by themselves are sufficient truth-makers. Hence we do not need states of affairs.

The Resemblance Nominalist analyzes *a*'s being F as a matter of resemblance relations holding between *a* and, say, suitable paradigm Fs. But that relation is also internal, dictated by what I called the particularized nature of *a* and the paradigm objects. Once again, states of affairs are not needed.

(But it seems that a Predicate Nominalist *will* require states of affairs. *a*'s being F is analyzed as *a*'s falling under the predicate F. But how can the falling under be dictated simply by *a* and the linguistic object F? Falling under is an external relation.)

Now for something very important. States of affairs have some rather surprising characteristics. Let us call *a, b*, F, R, et cetera, the constituents of states of affairs. It turns out that it is possible for there to be two different states of affairs that nevertheless have *exactly the same constituents*.

Here is a simple example. Let R be a nonsymmetrical relation (for instance, loves). Let it be the case, contingently, that *a* has R to *b* and *b* has R to *a*. Two distinct states of affairs exist: *a*'s having R to *b*, and *b*'s having R to *a* (*a*'s loving *b* and *b*'s loving *a*). Indeed, these states of affairs are *wholly* distinct, in the sense that it is possible for either state of affairs to fail to obtain while the other exists. Yet the two states of affairs have exactly the same constituents.

You can get the same phenomenon with properties as well as

relations (as pointed out by Lewis 1986c). Assume, as I think it is correct to assume, that a conjunction of states of affairs is itself a state of affairs. Then consider (1) $a$'s being F and $b$'s being G; and (2) $a$'s being G and $b$'s being F. Two wholly distinct states of affairs, it may be, but the very same constituents.

At this point, it is worth realizing that states of affairs may be required not simply by those who recognize universals but also by any philosophy that recognizes properties and relations, whether as universals or as particulars. This is very important, because we saw in examining Natural Class and Resemblance theories what difficulties there are in denying properties and relations (in espousing a blob view).

Suppose that $a$ has $R_1$ to $b$, with $R_1$ a particular, but a nonsymmetrical, relation. If $b$ has 'the same' relation to $a$, then, on a philosophy of tropes, we have $b$'s having $R_2$ to $a$: two states of affairs with different (though overlapping) constituents. For the loving that holds between $a$ and $b$ is a different object from the loving that holds between $b$ and $a$. Nevertheless $a$'s having $R_1$ to $b$ entails the existence of constituents $a$, $R_1$, and $b$, but the existence of these constituents does not entail that $a$ has $R_1$ to $b$. So states of affairs still seem to be something more than their constituents.

With tropes, you never get different states of affairs constructed out of exactly the same constituents. But given just one set of constituents, more than one state of affairs having just these constituents is *possible*. From $a$, trope $R_1$, and $b$, for instance, we could get $a$'s having $R_1$ to $b$ or $b$'s having $R_1$ to $a$. There is a way for a philosophy of tropes to avoid having to postulate states of affairs. But let us leave that aside until the next chapter.

I have spoken of the constituents of states of affairs. Could we also think and speak of them as *parts* of states of affairs? I think that it would be very unwise to think and speak of them in this way. Logicians have paid some attention to the notions of whole and part. They have worked out a formal calculus for manipulating these notions, which is sometimes called the calculus of individuals or, better, **mereology** (in Greek *meros* means a part). One philosopher who helped to work this out was Nelson Goodman, and in his book *The Structure of Appearance*, 1966, an account of mereology is given. There is one mereological principle that is very important for us here: If there are a number of things, and if they have a sum, that is, a whole of which they are parts, then they have just one sum.

I say *if* they have a sum, because it is controversial whether a number of things *always* have a sum. Do the square root of 2 and the Sydney Opera House have a sum? Philosophers differ on how permissive a mereology should be, that is, on whether there are limits to what you can sum, and if there are limits, where the limits fall. I myself would accept total permissiveness in summing. But all that is needed here is something that is agreed by all: where things can be summed, for each collection of things there is just one sum. We have just seen, however, that the complete constituents of a state of affairs are capable of being, and may actually even be, the complete constituents of a different state of affairs. Hence constituents do not stand to states of affairs as parts to whole.

It is worth noticing that complex universals have constituents rather than parts. At any rate this is so if we accept the Principle of Instantiation. Consider, for instance, conjunctive universals. If being P and Q is a conjunctive universal, then there must exist some particular, $x$, such that $x$ is both P and Q. But to say that is to say that there exists at least one state of affairs of the form $x$ is P and $x$ is Q. For the conjunctive universal to exist is for there to be a state of affairs of a certain sort. As a result, it is misleading to say that P and Q are *parts* of the conjunctive universal, a thing that I myself did say in the past (1978b, Ch. 15, Sec. II).

A very important type of complex universal is a *structural* property. A structural property involves a thing instantiating a certain pattern, such as a flag. Different parts (mereological parts) of the thing that instantiates the structural property will have certain properties. If the structural property involves relations, as a flag does, some or all of these parts will be related in various ways. It is easy to see that states of affairs must be appealed to. If *a* has P, and *b* has Q, and *a* has R to *b*, then and only then the object [*a* + *b*] has the structural property that may be presented in a shorthand way as P-R-Q.

A final point before leaving this particularly important section. The fact that states of affairs, if they exist, have a nonmereological mode of composition may have consequences for the theory examined in the previous chapter: the view that particulars are no more than bundles of universals. (I understand that this point comes from Mark Johnston.) We have seen that different states of affairs can have exactly the same constituents (*a*'s loving *b*, and *b*'s loving *a*). We have previously argued against the Bundle theory that two bundles containing exactly the same universals are impossible. They would be the very same bundle. Yet, considering the matter independently of the Bundle theory, why should not two different particulars be exactly alike? But now suppose that, as is plausible, we treat a bundling of universals as a state of affairs. Why should not exactly the same universals be bundled up in different ways?

In reply, I think it must be admitted that this is conceivable. But it would depend upon the Bundle theorist's working out a scheme that allowed for different bundling of the very same things. This is not provided for in the actual Bundle theories that have been developed. So if they want to take this path, then the onus is on Bundle theorists to try to develop their theory in a new way.

## V. A World of States of Affairs?

In the previous section it was argued that a philosophy that admits both particulars and universals ought to admit states of affairs (facts), which have particulars and universals as constituents (not as parts). As a matter of fact we saw that to introduce properties and relations at all, even as particulars, would apparently involve states of affairs. But our present concern is with universals.

The suggestion to be put forward now is that we should think of the world as a world of states of affairs, with particulars and universals only having existence within states of affairs. We have already argued for a Principle of Instantiation for universals. If this is a true principle, then the way is open to regard a universal as an identical element present in certain states of affairs. A particular that existed outside states of affairs would not be clothed in any properties or relations. It may be called a *bare* particular. If the world is to be a world of states of affairs we must add to the Principle of Instantiation a Principle of the Rejection of Bare Particulars.

This second principle looks plausible enough. In a Universals theory, it is universals that give a thing its nature, kind, or sort. A bare particular would not instantiate any universals, and thus would have no nature, be of no kind or sort. What could we make of such an entity? Perhaps a particular need not have any relations to any other particular—perhaps it could be quite isolated. But it must instantiate at least one property.

## VI. The Thin and the Thick Particular

Here is a problem that has been raised by John Quilter (1985). He calls it the "Antinomy of Bare Particulars." Suppose that particular *a* instantiates property F. *a* is F. This 'is' is obviously not the 'is' of identity, as in *a* is *a* or F is F. *a* and F are different entities, one being a particular, the other a universal. The 'is' we are dealing with is the 'is' of instantiation—of a fundamental tie between particular and property. But if the 'is' is not the 'is' of identity, then it appears that *a* considered in itself is really a bare particular lacking any properties. But in that case *a* has not got the property F. The property F remains outside *a*—just as transcendent forms remain outside the particular in Plato's theory.

I believe that we can at least begin to meet this difficulty by drawing the important distinction, already mentioned in Chapter 4, Section I, between the *thin* and the *thick* particular. The thin particular is *a*, taken apart from its properties (substratum). It is linked to its properties by instantiation, but it is not identical with them. It is not bare because to be bare it would have to be not instantiating any properties. But though clothed, it is thin.

However, this is not the only way that a particular can be thought of. It can also be thought of as involving its properties. Indeed, that seems to be the normal way that we think of particulars. This is the thick particular. But the thick particular, because it enfolds both thin particulars and properties, held together by instantiation, can be nothing but a state of affairs.

Suppose that *a* instantiates F, G, H, . . . They comprise the totality of *a*'s (nonrelational) properties. Now form the conjunctive property F&G&H. . . . Call this property N, where N is meant to be short for *a*'s nature. *a* is N is true, and *a*'s being N is a (rather complex) state of affairs. It is also the thick particular. *The thick particular is a state of affairs.* The properties of a thing are "contained within it" because they are constituents of this state of affairs. (Notice that states of affairs, such as *a*'s being N, are not repeatable. So, along with thin particulars, they can be called particulars also.)

Therefore, in one sense a particular is propertyless. That is the thin particular. In another sense it enfolds properties within itself. In the latter case it is the thick particular and is a state of affairs. I think that this answers the difficulty raised by the Antinomy of Bare Particulars.

Two points before leaving this section: First, the distinction between thin and thick particulars does not depend upon a doctrine of properties as universals. It does presuppose a substance-attribute account of a particular, rather than a bundle view. But we have already seen that it is possible to take a substance-attribute view with the attributes as particulars, that is, as tropes. The thin particular remains the particular with its attributes abstracted away. The thick particular is again a state of affairs: the thin particular's having the (particular) attributes that it has.

Second, the thin and the thick particular are really the two ends of a scale. In between is the particular clothed with some, but only some, of its properties. They may be properties that are, for one reason or another, particularly important. This intermediate particular will, of course, be a state of affairs, but a less comprehensive one than the state of affairs that is the thick particular.

## VII. Universals as Ways

The discussion in the previous section is not entirely satisfactory as it stands. It still leaves us with a picture of the thin particular and its properties as distinct metaphysical nodules that are linked together in states of affairs to form the thick particular. This makes the Principles of Instantiation and of the Rejection of Bare Particulars seem a bit arbitrary. Why must the nodules occur together? Could they not come apart? But would they then not be those unwanted creatures: uninstantiated universals and bare particulars?

Here I turn to a suggestion that has often been in the air, but had not, I think, been expounded systematically before David Seargent's book on Stout's theory of universals (1985). Unlike Stout, Seargent accepts universals, and in Chapter 4 he argues that we should think of them as *ways*. Properties are ways things are. The mass or charge of an electron is a way the electron is (in this case, a way that any electron is). Relations are ways things stand to each other.

If a property is a way that a thing is, then this brings the property into very intimate connection with the thing, but without destroying the distinction between them. One can see the point of thinking of instantiation as a fundamental connection, a tie or nexus closer than mere relation. Nor will one be much tempted by the idea of an uninstantiated property. A way that things are could hardly exist on its own.

Again, one will not be tempted by the idea that the way a thing stands to other things, a relation, could exist on its own, independent of the things. (Not that the idea was ever very tempting! It is easier to substantialize properties than relations.)

It may be objected that the phrases "ways things are" and "ways things stand to each other" beg the question against uninstantiated universals. Should I not have spoken of ways things could be and ways things could stand to each other, thus cancelling the implication that the ways must be the ways of actual things?

However, my argument is not attempting to take advantage of this semantic point. My contention is that once properties and relations are thought of not as things, but as ways, it is profoundly unnatural to think of these ways as floating free from things. Ways, I am saying, are naturally construed only as ways actual things are or ways actual things stand to each other. The idea that properties and relations can exist uninstantiated is nourished by the idea that they are not ways but things.

Before concluding this section, I should like to note that the conception of properties and relations as ways does not depend upon taking them as universals. We can still think of $a$'s property as a way that $a$ is, even if the property is particular, a trope. It will just be the case that no other thing besides $a$ can be that way. Similarly, a relation holding between $a$ and $b$ can still be a way $a$ and $b$ stand to each other, even if this way is nonrepeatable.

It is very important to realize that the notions of states of affairs and their constituents, the distinction between the thin and the thick particular, and the conception of properties and relations as ways things are and ways things stand to other things are available, if desired, to a philosophy of tropes as much as to a philosophy of universals.

## VIII. Multiple Location

To bring universals from a platonic realm down to earth, down to space-time, seems to involve saying something rather strange. It seems to follow that universals are, or may be, multiply located. For are they not to be found wherever the particulars that instantiate them are found? If two different electrons each have charge $e$, then $e$, one thing, a universal, is to be found in two different places, the places where the two electrons are, yet entirely and completely in each place. This has seemed wildly paradoxical to many philosophers.

Plato appears to be raising this difficulty in the *Philebus*, 15b-c. There he asked about a Form: "Can it be as a whole outside itself, and thus come to be one and identical in one thing and in several at once,—a view which might be thought to be the most impossible of all?" (trans. A. E. Taylor). A theory that kept universals in a separate realm from particulars would at least avoid this difficulty!

You might try just accepting the multiple location of universals. Some philosophers have. But then a difficulty can be raised: What about relations? Perhaps one can give *properties* a multiple location. But just where will you locate the "multiply located" relations? In the related things? That does not sound right. If $a$ precedes $b$ is the relation in both $a$ and $b$? Or in the thing $[a + b]$? Neither answer sounds right. But if it is not in the things, where is it?

I am inclined to meet the difficulty by saying that talk of the location of universals, while better than placing them in another realm, is also not quite appropriate. What should be said first, I think, is that the world is a world of states of affairs. These states of affairs involve particulars having properties and standing in relations to each other. The properties and relations are universals, which means both that different particulars can have the very same property and that different pairs, triples, . . . , of particulars can stand in the very same relation to each other. I do not think that all that is too startling a claim.

But if Naturalism is true, then the world is a single spatiotemporal manifold. What does this come to in terms of the states of affairs theory? That is, how do we reconcile Naturalism with the view sketched in the previous paragraph? It would be an enormous undertaking, presumably involving both fundamental science and philosophy, to give an answer involving even the sketchiest detail. All that can be said here is that the space-time world would have to be an enormous plurality or conjunction of states of affairs, with all the particulars that feature in the states of affairs linked up together (in states of affairs) by spatiotemporal relations.

To talk of locating universals in space-time then emerges as a crude way of speaking. Space-time is not a box into which universals are put. Universals are constituents of states of affairs. Space-time is a conjunction of states of affairs. In that sense universals are "in" space-time. But they are in it as helping to constitute it. I think that this is a reasonable understanding of *universalia in rebus*, and I hope that it meets Plato's objection. (For more on this topic see my *Can a Naturalist believe in Universals?* [1988a], together with critical comment in the same volume by Gilead Bar-Elli 1988.)


## IX. Higher-Order Types

We have seen that Class Nominalism and Resemblance Nominalism are in some difficulty with higher-order types: types whose tokens are themselves types. The difficulty is largely caused by the fact that these theories try to account for our talk about properties and relations without actually

99

allowing that there are any properties or relations. There is no such difficulty for a theory, such as the Universals theory, that admits properties and relations. But once we have properties and relations, possibilities open up. For now it is possible that these first-order properties and relations themselves have properties and relations.

Is it then being suggested that we should introduce *higher-order* properties and relations in order to explain higher-order types? Here we have to be very careful. Consider:

Redness is more like orange than it is like yellow.

One might take this as a second-order relation, of being more like than, which holds between three first-order universals. (Assuming they are universals, which can be disputed.) We have seen, however, that resemblance is an *internal* relation, one that flows necessarily from the nature of the terms. (Most philosophers would take the proposition above to be a necessary truth.)

In Section X of Chapter 3, however, I have already suggested that where we have internal relation, there we do not have anything ontologically extra over and above the related terms. The relation supervenes upon the terms: In every possible world that contains those terms, the relation holds. That, I think, makes the relation an ontological free lunch. But if that is so, we do not have any need to postulate a genuine higher-order relation.

Now many of the things that we want to say about properties and relations seem to be necessary truths. Consider red is a color, a meter is longer than a yard, being a mile distant from is a symmetrical relation. They all seem to be necessary truths. I am inclined to treat this necessity as giving us a clue that when we have a perspicuous account or analysis of these truths (no easy matter!), we shall not find any need to postulate higher-order properties and relations.

One very interesting internal relation that can hold between universals depends on these universals' being *complex*. We have noted that it is unwise to speak of universals having parts, because that suggests the part-whole relations studied by mereology. But complex universals do have constituents, and different universals may nevertheless contain the same constituent. A simple example is the complex properties P&Q and Q&R. Q is a common constituent of the two different properties. In virtue of these common constituents some complex universals may be said to be incompletely identical with each other.

I believe that these relations of incomplete identity between universals are of immense importance. In particular, they can be used to explain what *quantities* are. Consider the whole range of a quantity such as mass (an ounce in mass, a ton in mass, etc.). What unifies this class of universals, I suggest, are the incomplete identities holding between any two members of the class. But I leave development of this point aside for the present.

So do we ever need to postulate genuinely higher-order properties and relations of first-order properties and relations? For myself I believe that we do. In particular, we require relations between universals in order to give a satisfactory account of laws of nature. These should not be thought of, in the tradition of Hume, as mere regularities in the behavior of things. Rather, laws of nature are a matter of the presence of one property ensuring, or probabilifying, the presence of another. These are relations, external relations, contingent relations, holding between the one property and the other.

What of higher-order properties? I think that there may be need to postulate such properties in connection with the analysis of *functional* laws. But I cannot discuss this here. (See Armstrong 1983 for an account of laws of nature as relations between universals. Functional laws are discussed in Chapter 7 of that book.)

I will leave the topic of higher-order relations and properties of universals with this brief mention. What does require further discussion is the topic of the resemblance of universals. I will preface this, however, with a discussion of the formal properties of the relation of resemblance. We shall find that the Universals theory is very well placed to explain these formal properties.

## X. The Formal Properties of Resemblance

It will be remembered that the Resemblance Nominalist, for whom resemblance is a primitive notion, requires a series of special axioms for the characteristics of resemblance, axioms that he cannot justify but only state. (The Natural Class Nominalist equally requires special axioms for degrees of naturalness of classes.)

First, resemblance is symmetrical. If $a$ resembles $b$ to a certain degree, then $b$ resembles $a$ to just that degree. The upholder of universals can give a straightforward reductive explanation of this symmetry: It is simply the symmetry of identity. In the simplest case of resemblance, it is just a matter of common, that is, identical properties. However, a less simple case, it may be that $a$ and $b$ have no identical properties, yet have one or more *resembling* properties. I shall argue in the next section that in such a case the properties have common, that is, identical constituents. If that is correct, then the symmetry of resemblance of properties is again explained by the symmetry of identity.

If $a$ is exactly like $b$, and $b$ exactly like $c$, then $a$ must be exactly like $c$. Exact resemblance is not merely symmetrical: It is transitive. The Universals theory analyzes this situation by saying that $a$, $b$, and $c$ have exactly the same, the identical, properties. Identity is transitive.

We saw that the transitivity of exact resemblance is only a particular application of something more general. If $a$ resembles $b$ to some degree, and if $b$ exactly resembles $c$, then $a$ resembles $c$ to just the same extent that $a$ resembles $b$.

Resemblance of any degree is conserved under the substitution of exactly resembling objects. It is easy to see that this formal property will hold if resemblance always involves some identity of properties and that exact resemblance is identity of all properties.

Less than exact resemblance is not transitive. *a* can resemble *b* to a certain degree, *b* resemble *c* to the same degree, yet *a* fail to resemble *c* to that degree. Again the Universals theory explains the situation without the least difficulty. *a* and *b* have something identical, as have *b* and *c*. But because the identity is partial (incomplete) only, it need not be in the same (*identical*) respect. So transitivity fails for some, though not all, cases.

The Universals theory also explains why the notion of degrees of resemblance is so rough-and-ready. If resemblance is a matter of different identities in different cases, it is easy to see that degrees of resemblance will be a partially subjective matter, depending upon what particular properties we happen to be interested in, in the particular context. A Resemblance theory, on the contrary, just has to accept the rough-and-ready nature of resemblance as a primitive fact.

## XI. Resemblance Between Universals

Particulars, tokens, resemble each other in different degrees. The Universals theory begins, at least, by trying to analyze this in terms of common properties. But it seems that properties themselves resemble each other. Red, orange, and yellow all resemble each other: We group them together as colors. Triangularity and squareness resemble each other: They are both shapes. The ounce, the kilo, and the ton all resemble each other: They are all masses. Just as with resemblance of particulars, resemblance of properties admits of degree. Red is more like orange than it is like yellow. An ounce is more like a kilo than it is like a ton. These resemblances at the property level transfer themselves down to the first-order level of particulars. Other things being equal, a red thing is more like an orange thing than it is like a yellow thing.

In Section III of this chapter I discussed Wittgenstein's reflections on the word 'game' and other family-resemblance notions. I presented the following schematic picture of how a Universals theory might analyze such a situation:

| Particulars: | *a* | *b* | *c* | *d* | *e* |
|---|---|---|---|---|---|
| Their properties: | FGHJ | GHJK | HJKL | JKLM | KLMN |

We can now see this picture quite seriously underdescribes the typical situation. What contributes to resemblance-without-identity of the different sorts of thing covered by the one general word are resemblances-without-identity in the properties F, G, H, . . . For instance, all the objects falling under a certain general word may do so in virtue of having shape or mass. But they may have rather different sorts of shape and mass, so that the properties involved in applying the word are different in different cases, yet still have a likeness.

Here is an attractive preliminary way to think of the resemblance of universals. Many properties (colors, shapes, masses, etc.) fall into *orders*. (The orders may or may not be one dimensional.) The orders, which by and large are objective and not just a way that we happen to like arranging properties, are *resemblance* orders. Two properties that are close together in a certain order resemble each other closely. To be a color, say, is to be a property that lies in a certain resemblance order. Similarly for being a shape or a mass. You can work your way from one color to another via the close resemblance of intermediates. That is what makes the colors *colors*. It explains what we mean by saying, for instance, red is a color. The same goes for the shapes and masses, and so on.

Now because the relations involved are resemblance relations, they are internal relations, dictated by the nature of their terms. (I should argue that they are not something additional to the terms.) How shall we analyze the resemblance relations involved?

An analysis in the spirit of a Universals theory would be to appeal to common properties of the resembling things. This would involve common properties of properties: higher-order properties. However, although there seems to be no objection in principle to such a move, it is hard to see how such an analysis can be applied to the present cases. If the order considered contains many different properties to be ordered, as in the case of most quantities, huge numbers of higher-order properties would be required. We seem to have no independent grip on these properties besides their role in solving our present problem.

Perhaps then we should walk a bit towards a Resemblance theory? Chapter 3 showed it running into many difficulties. But that was because it rejected properties at the first-order level. We have got first-order properties now. Should we say that some of these first-order properties stand in unanalyzable resemblance relations to each other? Though unanalyzable, these relations of resemblance will have varying degrees of closeness. The resemblances will flow from the nature of the resembling universals. (Remember the particularized nature that I introduced in order to make Resemblance Nominalism as plausible as possible. But now we are appealing to the nature of universals.)

Such unanalyzable, primitive, resemblance of universals I regard as a fall-back position for the Realist about universals. It may in the end have to be accepted, at least for some cases. But it is an uncomfortable compromise, true to the superficial appearances, but lacking the deep attractiveness of a theory that always takes resemblance to involve some degree of identity.

A certain phenomenon noticed by one or two philosophers may provide us with encouragement. If we consider ordinary, first-order, particulars, then, as we noted in Chapter 4, two things, while remaining two, can resemble exactly. At least exact resemblance is possible (assuming that the Identity of Indiscernibles is not a necessary truth). In the limit, resemblance of particulars does not give identity. But now consider the resemblance of universals. As resemblance of properties gets closer and closer, we arrive in the limit at identity. Two become one. This suggests that as resemblance gets closer, more and more constituents of the resembling properties are identical, until all the constituents are identical and we have identity rather than resemblance.

Here is a working out of this idea in a simple case: Consider the property of being just five kilograms in mass. For something to have that property the thing must consist of two parts, parts with no overlap between them, such that one part is just four kilos in mass, the other just one. It is a simple form of structural property, simple because no special relations are needed between the two parts: The parts can be scattered parts. We can use the language of states of affairs. The state of affairs of something's being a five-kilo object is the conjunction of two states of affairs: something's being four kilos plus something else's (nonoverlapping something else) being a one-kilo state of affairs.

We can now understand the (reasonably close) resemblance between the properties being five kilos in mass and being four kilos in mass. (We can also see clearly, incidentally, why no object can have both these properties at the same time.) Being five kilos in mass involves the five-kilo thing having a part, a proper part to put it technically, that is four kilos in mass. (Moreover, a thing that is four kilos in mass can never be more than a proper part of a five-kilo object.) The properties resemble because a four-kilo object is a large proportion of a five-kilo object. The bigger the part, the closer to identity, and so the closer the resemblance.

My idea is that in this or similar ways, the resemblances holding between properties can be explained. Resembling properties are never simple properties. Different simple properties never resemble, at any rate in the absence of common higher-order properties. Resembling properties are complex properties, their complexity established by logical analysis or, more likely, empirical, scientific, identification. The complexity will regularly involve structures, with the parts of the things having the property themselves having properties and, perhaps, standing in relations to other parts. Thus, the "soundiness" of sound is to be identified with a suitable wave structure of a suitable medium. Resemblances between sounds are to be spelled out in terms of resemblances between their wave structures, ultimately getting down to such things as length, which can be treated in the same way as that indicated for mass.

(Hume thought that different simple properties *can* resemble. In the *Treatise*, Bk. I, Pt. I, Sec. VII, note, he wrote:

'Tis evident, that even different simple ideas may have a similarity or resemblance to each other; nor is it necessary, that the point or circumstance of resemblance shou'd be distinct or separable from that in which they differ. *Blue* and *green* are different simple ideas, but are more resembling than *blue* and *scarlet*; tho' their perfect simplicity excludes all possibility of separation or distinction.

Hume, in effect, is here upholding primitive resemblance between properties. I would argue against him that the color properties have a concealed complexity, a complexity that nevertheless operates upon us to produce an awareness of resemblance. Hume's view that "simple ideas" must be as they appear to be, namely, simple, would prevent him from accepting this.)

Whether this program can be carried through or not, it is an appealing idea that we can get rid of primitive resemblances between universals. But there are some quite formidable difficulties. My most recent attempt to advance the program can be found in a paper "Are Quantities Relations?" (1988b).

## XII. The Fundamental Tie

What of the need for a fundamental tie—the tie or nexus of instantiation? Many people have thought it an overwhelming difficulty for a theory of universals. I do not think that the problem of characterizing the nature of the tie should detain us. This was Plato's concern in the first part of his *Parmenides*. There he showed conclusively that the relation of particular to form cannot be either "participation" or "imitation." But it is perfectly reasonable for an upholder of universals to claim that instantiation is a primitive that cannot be explicated by any analysis, definition, or metaphor. Nevertheless, the upholder of universals can go on to say, we all understand what it is to judge or even just to perceive that a particular has a property or that a relation holds between two or more terms. After all, the Natural Class theory takes the notion of a natural class as primitive and the Resemblance Nominalist does the same with the relation of resemblance. Why not instantiation as a directly apprehended primitive?

The problem is rather the regress that seems to be involved. The particular *a* instantiates property F. Prima facie, however, instantiation is a universal, found wherever there are things having properties. So this state of affairs, *a*'s instantiating property F, is a token of the type *instantiation* (but dyadic instantiation now). The state of affairs instantiates instantiation. But here we have another token of instantiation. So the state of affairs (that state of affairs instantiating instantiation) also instantiates instantiation. And so on ad infinitum. The regress that results is either vicious or at least viciously uneconomical.

This regress I have called in the past the relation regress. It could also be called the fundamental tie regress or nexus regress. It takes the fundamental tie patronized by particular solutions to the Problem of Universals. It then applies that solution to the particular tie and attempts to deduce a regress.

The Natural Class theory uses class membership as the

nexus; the Resemblance Nominalist uses primitive resemblance. In Section XI of Chapter 3 I tried to answer the nexus-regress argument as it was deployed by Russell against the Resemblance theory. I suggested that what saved the Resemblance theory was that resemblance is an internal relation, dictated by the nature of its terms, the resembling things. Internal relations, it is plausible to hold, are nothing over and above their terms. The same holds for resemblances between resemblance situations, and so on. But if so, I argued, the regress is as harmless as, say, the truth regress.

The same holds for class membership. Given $a$ and given $\{a, \ldots\}$ the relation of class membership supervenes. Hence, it seems, the regress is not to be feared. No ontological regress, no need to postulate an infinity of extra entities (with each bringing up the same old problem).

But in general at least and perhaps in every case, the fact that an object instantiates a certain property does not flow from the nature of the object and the nature of the universal that are involved. The connection is contingent. And if an object is related to another object and that relation is external, the same point holds. So it may seem that, unlike the cases of resemblance and class membership, the regress of instantiation goes through.

However, my idea is that the instantiation regress can be halted after one step. We have to allow the introduction of a fundamental tie or nexus: instantiation. But suppose that we have that $a$ instantiates F or that $a$ and $b$ in that order instantiate R. Do we have to advance any further? I do not think that we do. For note that the alleged advance is now, as it was not at the first step, logically determined by the postulated states of affairs. If $a$ instantiates F and instantiation is a universal-like entity, then we are logically forced to say that $a$, F, and instantiation instantiate instantiation, and so on. But perhaps we can allow this while denying that to "$a$, F, and instantiation instantiating instantiation" any extra state of affairs in the world corresponds. As we go on expanding the regress, our statements remain true, but no new truth-maker, or ontological ground, is required for all these statements to be true.

I do not feel totally secure about this answer. But suppose that it is unsatisfactory. Will not that unsatisfactoriness also reopen the question of the other two regresses, the class and the resemblance regress? If the obtaining of instantiation must be analyzed in terms of instantiation, will it not be fair to insist that the holding of class membership must be analyzed in terms of classes and the relation of resemblance must be analyzed in terms of resemblances? And what theory then will escape the whipping? As Berkeley pointed out on a number of occasions, what is an objection to all theories equally does nothing to favor some over others.

A very important final point. In Section IV of this chapter we encountered the notion of states of affairs, with (thin) particulars and universals as the constituents of states of affairs. But we said that a's being F is something more than just its constituents a and F. It may now be seen that in talking about states of affairs and talking about instantiation, we are talking about the same phenomenon. The state of affairs of a's being F exists if and only if a instantiates F because these are two ways of talking about the same thing. Similarly, if R is a symmetrical relation, then a's having R to b is the same thing as a and b instantiating R. If R is nonsymmetrical or asymmetrical, then the situation is a little more complex. There are two possible states of affairs that can both be rendered as a and b instantiating R: a's having R to b and b's having R to a. That, indeed, suggests that talking about states of affairs is a simpler and more perspicuous way of talking than talking about instantiation. The *fundamental tie*, or *nexus*, in a Universals theory is nothing but the bringing together of particulars and universals in states of affairs.

### XIII. The Apparatus of an
### Attribute Theory of Universals

The Universals theory, in its subject-attribute form, requires a reasonably comprehensive ontology to account for the objective existence of natural classes. First, it countenances properties and relations. However, in view of the great difficulties posed by theories that try to construct properties and relations out of other materials, this is perhaps prudence rather than extravagance. Second, it accepts the existence of states of affairs. These are complex entities having constituents, but these constituents differ from the parts of wholes treated by the calculus of whole and part. It is true that any recognition of properties and relations, even as particulars, as tropes, will apparently involve states of affairs. But the rules of composition for possible states of affairs that involve only tropes are somewhat nearer to the rules for whole and part. (For instance, if R is a nonsymmetrical relation, a Universals theory has the possibility of two wholly distinct states of affairs: $aRb$ and $bRa$ composed of the very same constituents. With tropes the two Rs could not be identical. Given $a$, trope R', and $b$, one might have $aR'b$ or $bR'a$ but not both, although one could have, for example, $aR'b$ and $bR''a$.)

The Universals theory requires the notion of the instantiation of a property, the instantiation of a dyadic relation, or a triadic relation, . . . or of an n-adic relation. (If what universals there are is a contingent matter, not to be settled a priori, then not all these sorts of instantiation need actually exist.) But notice that the trope theory, in its subject-attribute form, also requires monadic, dyadic, triadic, . . . fundamental ties. By contrast, a Bundle theory of tropes does not require a monadic tie (it substitutes the dyadic compresence of properties), but it still requires dyadic, triadic, . . . relations *between* bundles.

But as we have noticed, a Universals theory does not require both states of affairs and a set of fundamental ties. To have one is to have the other. The Universals theory may require a primitive notion of degrees of resemblance holding between universals. This seems a quite heavy extra commitment for the theory. As a result, a good deal may hang on whether this sort of resemblance can be analyzed in terms of overlap of constituents of the resembling universals.

# CHAPTER SIX

# Tropes

## I. Substances Versus Bundles

We now turn to consider theories that admit properties and relations, but admit them as particulars. It is possible to admit such properties and relations, yet allow them in turn to instantiate universal properties and relations. But as has already been noted, this position is not of great interest. Here, except for a brief final section, we confine ourselves to Nominalist versions of the Trope theory.

I have adopted the term *trope* with some hesitation. The trouble is not a lack of names but a superabundance of them. What has happened, I think, is that in many cases the tropes kept being discovered anew by philosophers. Then, unaware that the theory was already an old and respectable one, each philosopher had to make up a name for them. So we have "abstract particulars" (Stout 1921, Campbell 1981), "perfect particulars" (Bergmann 1967), "tropes" (D. C. Williams 1966), "cases" (Wolterstorff 1970), "concrete properties" (Küng 1967— he calls universals "abstract properties"), "unit-properties" (Matthews and Cohen 1968), "property-instances" (various philosophers). The term *trope* is catching on a bit, so I have

---

It is suggested that D. C. Williams's "The Elements of Being," K. K. Campbell's "The Metaphysic of Abstract Particulars," and C. B. Martin's "Substance Substantiated" be used as companion readings to this chapter.

decided to follow Williams's usage. (Williams, a good scholar, was probably aware of the problem of a name.)

We have already noted that a Trope theory can choose between Substance-attribute theories of particulars and a Bundle theory. On the former view, particulars *have* properties and stand in relations to other particulars. The properties and relations are particulars, but that need be the only difference from a substance-attribute view that works with universals.

In modern times Trope theories have generally been developed as bundle theories. Here Stout, Williams, and Campbell constitute a line of succession. In each case we find worries about the mysteriousness of particulars considered in abstraction from properties and relations, together with exhilaration at the thought that the whole world can be constructed from tropes. Particulars *reduce* to bundles of compresent tropes. Relation tropes can then relate such bundles.

A bundle-of-tropes view of particulars has a great advantage over a bundle-of-universals account. We saw Russell developing the latter view in terms of a relation of compresence that holds between universals. But the relation, although symmetrical, is not transitive, and such a relation is not very suitable when it comes to constructing nonoverlapping bundles. However, if it is tropes that we want to bundle, then the situation is a good deal easier. Tropes are not identical across different particulars, as universals are, thus the fundamental compresence relation can be taken to be both symmetrical and transitive. It then catches all *and only* the tropes in one particular, which is just the result wanted.

Nevertheless, as between a bundle-of-tropes account of particulars and a substance-attribute view with the attributes as tropes, I think that the latter view is superior. This is the view upheld by C. B. Martin (1980), following his hero Locke.

An objection against the bundle view is that the tropes are not really suited to be the substances of the world. The point seems fairly obvious in the case of relations. Substances are capable of independent existence. But could, say, a "between-ness" exist on its own, a relation without any terms? The idea seems ridiculous, whether the betweenness is a universal or a particular.

A Trope theorist may not wish to treat relations as substances, giving this role to properties only. Yet even when we turn to *property* tropes, it is not clear that we have entities that can serve as substances. In discussing the view that particular things are bundles of universals (Chapter 4, Section IV), I said that such properties as particular mass and charge—natural candidates for universals—do not seem to be at all suitable to be the substance of the world. They could not exist independent of anything else. But the substitution of tropes for universals may not improve the situation much. A trope of a particular mass or particular charge seems nearly as insubstantial, as incapable of independent existence, as the corresponding universal.

Evidence that tropes are not well fitted to be "junior substances" (a neat phrase that A. J. Ayer applied to the sense data that he thought were involved in all perception) is to be found in the way that Trope theorists who are also Bundle theorists try to build up tropes into something a little bit more substantial. They tend to give them spatial and temporal characteristics: shape, size, and duration. In this way the trope is swelled up a bit. Yet the theorists are then embarrassed because shape, size, and duration appear themselves to be properties and therefore ought to be tropes themselves alongside other property tropes.

David Lewis has suggested to me that the Trope theorist who is also a Bundle theorist should offer as his junior substances simple properties (an ultimate quantum of mass, say), which exist at a point and for an instant only. One could object that these substances were still being given spatial and temporal characteristics (they are pointlike and instantlike), so that the simple property would still not be existing on its own. I suppose that the reply to this would be that what makes these atoms "at a point" and "at an instant" is simply the relations, spatial and temporal, that the atoms have to other atoms. In themselves, the atoms are just simple property tropes. Duration, size, shape, et cetera, are just networks of atoms in relation. A minimal mass trope on its own would not have any spatial or temporal characteristics.

No doubt this is the best that can be done for the view that tropes are the sole substance of the world. One disadvantage is that it commits the Trope theorist to something that is rather controversial: that a purely relational account of space and time is true. But if this consequence is satisfactory, I do not have a further argument against the bundle-of-tropes view, although I remain suspicious of it.

If tropes are not the substance of the world, then it seems that one should adopt a position like C. B. Martin's. Property tropes are properties, attributes, *of* particulars. Relation tropes are relations holding between particulars. This, I believe, should be combined with the recognition that the tropes are not things at all, except in the very widest sense of the word 'thing', where it means no more than 'entity'. Following Seargent, I advocated taking universals as ways: ways that things are in themselves (properties) and ways that things stand to each other (relations). (See Chapter 5, Section VII.) I see no reason why a trope theory should not also conceive of its properties and relations as ways. They would be particularized ways, with no more than a resemblance, close or less close, to other particularized ways. I take it to be an advantage of this view that properties and relations are treated in parallel fashion.

## II. States of Affairs Again

It was argued in the previous chapter that a Universals theory is committed to states of affairs (facts). It seems that a Trope theory, whether in a bundle or a substance-attribute version, must also admit states of affairs. The states of affairs involving tropes do not obey quite the same rules as those involving universals. The Universals theory works with states of affairs that, taken all together, have fewer constituents. This is because one universal does the work of many tropes. But both types of theory require states of affairs.

Thus, suppose that $a$ has property trope F. This is either a matter of F's standing in the bundling relation to the other tropes that make up $a$ (bundle version) or else is a matter of F's being an attribute of $a$ (substance-attribute version). In either case, states of affairs are required. For instance, $a$'s being F entails the existence of $a$ and trope F. But $a$ and trope F could exist without $a$'s being F. So $[a + F]$ (the object that is the mere sum of $a$ and F) is an insufficient truth-maker for $a$'s being F. States of affairs are required as part of the ontology of any trope theory. See Section IV of Chapter 5 for the general line of argument.

If the argument of the foregoing paragraph is accepted, then all layer-cake theories, theories that admit properties and relations, require states of affairs. Blob theories, by contrast, whether in a natural class or a resemblance version, do not. The reason is that the latter theories try to unify the world and furnish truth-makers for true statements by means of class membership or resemblance relations. These fundamental ties are internal, which means that they are not something that is an ontological addition to the terms of the relation. Hence they can dispense with states of affairs. However, this ontological economy is completely outweighed by the implausibility of not admitting properties and relations into the ontological count.

However, as I have recently become aware, there is a way in which trope theories can avoid having to postulate states of affairs. In private communication, C. B. Martin, who is a Trope theorist, has argued that properties of things and relations between things are *nontransferable*. Suppose that $a$ has trope F or that $a$ has R to $b$. Martin does not claim that

117

it is a necessary truth that $a$ has F or has R to $b$. But granted that F and R exist, which is not necessary, then he says that it is a necessary truth that they could not have been attached to, or hold between, anything else. They are essentially the F of $a$ or the R that $a$ has to $b$. This is not just the way that we would naturally describe them. It is the way that they have to be.

It follows that in a world that contains $a, b$, F, and R, then that world also contains $a$'s being F and $a$'s having R to $b$. States of affairs flow necessarily from, supervene on, the bare existence of their constituents. Hence we need not assume that states of affairs are anything additional to their constituents. They become an ontological free lunch.

What should we think of getting rid of states of affairs by postulating necessities in this way? Much will depend upon what view one takes of the metaphysics of modality: the theory of necessity and contingency. My own approach to modality is combinatorial. In Armstrong 1989 I argue for the following general approach: Possibilities that are not actual are given by any recombination of the elements of states of affairs (these elements being thin particulars, properties, and relations) in a way that respects the form of states of affairs. If one takes this approach to possibility, then one will see no reason why property tropes and relation tropes should not be shifted around promiscuously to yield possible states of affairs.

Even if one does not accept such an account of possibility, it seems that to postulate these necessities is to trade in one bulge in the carpet for another. States of affairs have their cost: One has to accept that it is at least possible that different states of affairs contain exactly the same constituents. Martin's necessities have their cost also: Given the world's particulars, properties, and relations, then the nature of the world is ineluctably fixed. A rather mysterious necessity in the world. Which poison should the boys in the backroom choose?

Another matter before concluding this section. In expounding the theory of universals it was argued that, as against a priori realism, it is not necessary that we postulate a universal corresponding to each general word. The relations between *predicates that truly apply to something* and *universals that things instantiate* is never a simple one. Instead I suggested that it ought to be established a posteriori, on the basis of scientific considerations, just what universals there are.

The same can be said about the tropes. There is, for instance, no more reason to assume that each of the tokens of *game* involve an exactly or nearly resembling trope of gamehood than there is reason for a Universals theory to assume a universal of gamehood. We can perfectly well have what David Lewis calls a *sparse* theory of tropes as much as a sparse theory of universals.

## III. Tropes and the Problem of Universals

Our central concern, though, is with the Problem of Universals. Let there be property and relation tropes, but no universals. Suppose that two objects have exactly the same mass. Associated with each object will be different mass tropes. We will want to think of them as both mass M tropes, where M takes some determinate value. But what is our warrant for this? If we exclude the rather feeble answer that both tropes fall under the same predicate (what trope analysis could we give of 'falling under the same predicate'?), only two answers seem plausible. First, the class of mass M tropes form a primitively natural class; second, the class of mass M tropes is a class of exactly resembling things, with resemblance a primitive. In other words, in the absence of universals we must either try a trope version of the Natural Class theory, or a trope version of Resemblance Nominalism (positions IV and V in the diagram in Chapter 1, Section III).

The natural class view was held by G. F. Stout. We have

seen that he accepted the Trope theory in a bundle form. For him "abstract particulars," as he called them, fell into "classes or kinds" that have a "distributive unity." He explained that the distributive unity of class or kind of abstract particulars is *not* determined by their resemblance. Rather, that resemblance is determined by the distributive unity of the class or kind (1921, p. 387 in the 1930 reprinting). This makes it clear that Stout's view is like Quinton's natural class view, but one that works with tropes rather than ordinary particulars. Stout's view is a layer-cake view, Quinton's is a blob view, and I think that Stout has the advantage because of this.

The alternative view, that the unity of classes of tropes is based upon the primitive and unanalyzable notion of resemblance, was upheld by D. C. Williams in his classic paper, "The Elements of Being" (1966). Keith Campbell follows him in another fine paper, "The Metaphysic of Abstract Particulars" (1981). As both titles hint, these papers take a bundle view of particulars. (See also Campbell's *Abstract Particulars*, forthcoming, which develops his view into a whole ontology.)

In my estimation, the resemblance version of the trope theory is considerably superior to the natural class variant. However, as I have already said, I believe that a substance-attribute account, as in C. B. Martin's "Substance Substantiated" (1980), is to be preferred to a bundle view.

In my earlier work on universals (1978), I underestimated the strength of a tropes + resemblance (+ substance-attribute) view. In my present estimation, out of the six main positions on the Problem of Universals set forth in the diagram in Chapter 1, Section III, it is a close second to the first choice, which is a Realism about universals (also in a substance-attribute form). As race commentators in Australia say, daylight is third, although, for the record, I think of Stout's view as leading the rest of the pack home.

As we shall now see, when the natural class and the resemblance views are deployed in a new context, the context of tropes, a lot of things change. Here is a first difference. In the original Natural Class theory we have a top of the scale: a class with the highest degree of distributive unity. With orthodox Resemblance Nominalism we also have a top of the scale: things that perfectly resemble each other. However, and this is a vital point, in both cases the top of the scale is rather theoretical. Only perhaps in the submicroscopic realm do we get perfect twins, perfectly resembling things.

The situation changes in a very interesting way when it comes to tropes. Consider charge $e$ that each electron has and that is supposed to be exactly the same for all electrons. Now consider the class of $e$ tropes. (It includes tropes that are not associated with electrons, in particular, I am informed, tropes of muons.) It is a natural class with the highest possible degree of unity. Or in the language of the Resemblance theory, it is a class of tropes, each of which resembles the other exactly.

This is no isolated example. Consider any precise degree of any quantity, or exact shade of any color, or any exact shape. The corresponding tropes will resemble exactly. Of course, we throw away the fact that they are set in environments that fail to resemble exactly. Internally, we have exact resemblance, or in Stoutian terms, the highest degree of distributive unity.

## IV. Tropes as Substitutes for Universals

Now consider the whole field of tropes, every one that there is. This field can be divided up into mutually exclusive classes, each of which is an exact resemblance class, a class with the highest degree of natural unity. This can be seen as soon as it is remembered that exact resemblance is symmetrical, transitive, and reflexive. A relation with those features will divide up a field into bundles, that is, into mutually exclusive, nonoverlapping, classes. Of course, there will very likely be singleton classes (unit classes). These will correspond to the cases that a Universals theory would speak of as situations where a universal is only instantiated once. These mutually exclusive classes now serve as an excellent substitute for universals: as ersatz universals.

A universal has a certain extension: the class of all the particulars that instantiate that universal. In the Trope theory, the same particulars will fail to instantiate a universal, but will as a substitute have a trope. The class of these tropes will be a class of exactly resembling tropes. Furthermore, it will be, as the logicians say, closed under exact resemblance. That is, the class cannot be expanded any further without creating a failure of exact resemblance.

So for each instantiated universal, a class of exactly corresponding tropes can be postulated as a substitute. The correspondence also goes the other way. To each class of exactly resembling tropes, a universal can be postulated as a substitute. So provided you abandon uninstantiated universals (good riddance, I say), and provided Universals theorists and Trope theorists coordinate their views on just what properties and relations the world contains, it is easy to pass back and forth between the theories.

This is all rather nice business for the Trope theory, especially if you are suspicious of universals. You get a construction that will do almost all the work that universals do, without having to postulate them. Paradise on the cheap!

## V. A Trope Substitute for the Resemblance of Universals

So tropes can fill in for universals. Wherever the Universals theory postulates a universal, the Trope theory can substitute an equivalence class of exactly resembling tropes. Equally, of course, wherever the Trope theory postulates an equivalence class of exactly resembling tropes, the Universals theory can substitute a universal. (This result could also be presented in terms of natural classes of tropes having the highest degree of naturalness or distributive unity. But the resemblance presentation seems more perspicuous.)

We have seen that, from the standpoint of a Universals theory, it is natural to say that not only do ordinary particulars resemble each other, but that there is (inexact) resemblance between the universals themselves. The different mass properties resemble each other in being mass properties, the different colors resemble in being colors. Red resembles orange more than it resembles yellow. It now turns out that the tropes yield a perfectly good substitute for this resemblance of universals.

The point turns on one of the formal properties of resemblance that we have already noted (Chapter 3, Section I). If $a$ resembles $b$ to some degree, D, then just this degree of resemblance holds if an exactly resembling particular is substituted for $a$ or for $b$. Resemblance to degree D is conserved under such substitutions. Now, instead of ordering universals in terms of their resemblance to each other, we want to order their substitutes: classes of exactly resembling tropes. Presumably we can assume that the formal properties of resemblance do not change in moving from ordinary particulars to tropes. Imagine, then, that just one trope is selected at random from each equivalence class of exactly resembling tropes. Form a class of these selections. This class is exactly correlated with the class of universals. And the (inexact) resemblance between the tropes in this class will exactly mirror whatever inexact resemblance there may be between the universals.

Consider three universals: a certain exact shade of red, a certain exact shade of orange, and a certain exact shade of yellow. The first resembles the second more than the first resembles the third. We have already seen that this does not necessarily hold for ordinary things (Chapter 2, Section VIII). The red thing's resemblance to the orange thing in respect of color might be outweighed by the existence of many resemblances in other respects between the red and the yellow thing. But now consider three corresponding tropes. The red trope, we can be certain, will resemble the orange trope more than it resembles the yellow trope. For the red, orange, and yellow tropes correlate exactly with the corresponding universals. We can repeat this result for the whole realm of universals.

We have been working with resemblance here. It seems that the same results are available to a natural class version of the Trope theory. Consider the class containing just one red and just one orange trope. Compare it with a class containing that red trope and just one yellow trope. Neither class has the highest degree of distributive unity. But it seems reasonable to say that the first class has a *higher* degree of distributive unity than the second class. (We saw in Chapter 2, Section VIII, that this could break down for ordinary particulars. But it is secure in the case of tropes because they are so "thin.") The Natural Class theorist can then identify the resemblance of tropes with this higher degree of distributive unity, thus gaining the result desired.

A Trope theory can thus exhibit (inexact) resemblance among types as an (inexact) resemblance between tropes rather than inexact resemblance between universals. The resemblance of universals is a puzzling phenomenon for a Universals theory because in many cases the resemblance seems to be primitive, thus saddling the Universals theory with some irreducible resemblances. But irreducible resemblance would not worry the Trope theorist. Some tropes resemble each other exactly, so yielding a trope counterpart of "instantiating the same universal." Others resemble inexactly, thus yielding a trope counterpart of "the resemblance of universals."

In Chapter 5, Section XI, I suggested that resemblance of universals might be explained in terms of partial identity of the constituents of the universals concerned. That is a program for research that I think is hopeful, but that may possibly have to be abandoned. The Trope theorist can take a delightfully relaxed attitude toward this program. If it succeeds, he can model its success in his tropes. He will turn it into a matter of exact similarity holding between some, but only some, of the constituents of complex tropes. (Or if the notion of a complex trope is rejected, it can be taken to be a matter of some of the constituents of a complex of tropes being exactly similar.)

It may be even better from the Trope theorist's point of view if the attempt to analyze the resemblance of universals fails for at least some cases. He will model this by an inexact resemblance of tropes *not* based on the exact resemblance of constituents of the tropes in question. He never claimed to analyze resemblance (except perhaps in terms of distributive unity). So why should he not allow that primitive resemblance (or distributive unity) has degrees?

## VI. Trope Nominalism Versus "Regular" Nominalism

So the philosophy of tropes is riding high. In this section it continues to ride quite high as we explore advantages that it has over orthodox Nominalism, together with some possible disadvantages. We will not be greatly concerned with the distinction between a Natural Class theory of tropes and a Resemblance view.

First, there is the coextension problem. It seems possible that two wholly distinct properties should nevertheless be coextensive, qualifying the very same particulars. How is this to be explained by a regular Nominalism? As we saw (Chapter 2, Section III, and Chapter 3, Section VIII) there seems to be no explanation available, because the things involved lack any property structure. In that respect, they are blobs. No wedge can be pushed between the properties.

This difficulty, we saw, is no difficulty for a Universals

theory. Equally, however, it is no difficulty for a Trope theory. Let P and Q be distinct but coextensive properties. Given a trope analysis of the situation, P-tropes and Q-tropes are perfectly distinct, even if neither is ever found except in the presence of the other.

Second, since there can be relation tropes as well as property tropes, there will be no call for an elaborate and unconvincing analysis of relations in terms of ordered classes of particulars (or unordered classes of unordered classes if the Wiener-Kuratowski device for getting rid of ordered classes is used), which regular or blob nominalisms find forced upon them. There will simply be the relations, taken as particulars, themselves relating particulars, and standing in relations of exact or less then exact resemblance to other particularized relations. This last relation of resemblance will be an internal one, and thus not something that constitutes an ontological addition.

Third, once properties and relations are admitted, even if only as particulars, then the way is open, if one should so wish or require, to introduce properties and relations *of* these first-order properties and relations. We have already noted, in Chapter 5, Section IX, that a statement's appearing to say something about a property or relation does not automatically require us to postulate further properties and relations of the original ones. To argue from language to higher-order properties is a very a priori manner of proceeding. The statements may and often, I think, do permit of an analysis that avoids such ontological expense. Nonetheless, the facts may turn out to be such that we do want to attribute properties and relations to properties and relations. A philosophy of tropes can permit such an attribution.

One interesting difference does then emerge between tropes and universals. Let *a* have P' and *b* have P", where P' and P" are two exactly resembling tropes. Contrast this with a universals analysis, where *a* has P, *b* has P, and P = P. On a trope view, it would seem possible for P' to have a higher-order property Q', whereas P" lacks any exactly similar higher-order property Q". The apparent possibility is created because we are dealing with particulars the whole time. But it would not be possible for the *universal* P to have Q in one instantiation and lack Q in another. P "in one instantiation" and P "in another" do not differ. P is one and the same thing in each instantiation. So it cannot both have Q and lack Q. I do not have any clear opinion as to whether this gives the Trope theory some advantage, by allowing more flexibility, or whether the possibility opened up is so arcane that the theory that eliminates it—the Universals theory—has the advantage.

### VII. Bundles Versus Substance-Attribute Again

There is another interesting point about properties (as opposed to relations) of trope properties and trope relations. We have noted that a Trope theory may be held in a bundle-of-properties or else in a substance-attribute form. Although the bundle view is orthodoxy among Trope theorists, and although it seems superior to the bundle-of-universals account, it was suggested that Trope theorists do better to embrace Locke's and C. B. Martin's substance-attribute version.

The possibility that first-order properties and relations might themselves have properties seems an additional point in favor of a Substance-Attribute theory. What would it be for a first-order trope to have a property? Should we say that a first-order trope is nothing but a bundle of its properties? Such a view seems very unattractive. A substance-attribute model of the relation of a first-order trope to its property seems much the more inviting. It is interesting to note that Russell went this way when he developed his Bundle-of-universals theory of particulars. He wrote: "I should regard 'red is a colour' as a genuine subject-predicate proposition, assigning to the 'substance' *red* the quality *colour*" (1959, p. 171). But if a substance-attribute view is preferable at the second level, then this seems to be some argument for embracing it even at the first level.

### VIII. Natural Classes of Tropes Versus Resemblance

The object of this section is to argue that, as between a natural class and a resemblance version of Trope Nominalism, the resemblance version is to be preferred. First, we go back to Wolterstorff's argument (Chapter 2, Section IV), which was brought against the "regular" version of the Natural Class theory. The argument is based upon the identity conditions for classes: They are identical if and only if their members are identical. Different members, different classes. Because of this, if to have a certain property is to be a member of a class, then had the class been different, the property would have been different. But the conclusion seems unacceptable. The property might have been no different. So, it appears, properties are independent of classes.

If this argument is good, then it seems unaffected by the substitution of a natural class of tropes for a natural class of ordinary particulars. However, it appears that the argument does not affect a resemblance version of a trope view. Consider a class of exactly resembling tropes, say the class of five-kilograms-exact tropes. What matters about the class is that it is closed under exact resemblance. That is to say, the class contains all and only the tropes that exactly resemble each other "in this respect."

Because the relation of resemblance is an internal one, it will depend upon the particularized nature of each trope. We have already met with the notion of a particularized nature (Chapter 3, Section II), but there it was a "thick" particularized nature, a substitute for the totality of the properties of an ordinary thing. There I was inclined to say that we should distinguish between a thing and its particularized nature. But for tropes, it seems natural to say that the trope *is* its particularized nature.

We need one trope from the resemblance class to identify the class. But having got such a trope, the rest of the class is assembled according to a general principle: whatever tropes exactly resemble this trope. As a result, it is possible that there should be more or fewer of these exactly resembling tropes. The natural class view, however, starts and finishes with the whole class, giving no analysis of its structure. So it is stuck with the whole class and cannot answer Wolterstorff's argument.

Second, I argued that we place a thing in a certain natural class because it has a certain property, rather than attributing a certain property to it because it is a member of a certain class. Class views of properties get the direction of explanation wrong (Chapter 2, Section V). This argument, a close relative of Wolterstorff's, also seems to be unaffected by substituting classes of tropes for classes of ordinary particulars.

A similar argument may be mounted against a resemblance view. It may be argued that it is not the resemblance of things that determine their properties (the same resemblance pattern might flow from different properties) but rather that the properties of things determine their resemblance. Consider, in particular, a thing alone in the universe, thus resembling nothing. It can still have properties.

In the case of a Resemblance theory that does not admit tropes, this argument's force was at least blunted by the doctrine of a particularized nature from which resemblances flow. The resemblances become secondary to these natures. Resemblances can even be absent as in the case of the thing alone in the universe. Just as in the Universals theory, resemblance is taken to be secondary, but secondary now to the particularized nature of the resembling things. Hence a resemblance view can agree that resemblances are secondary.

This reply seems to work even better with the tropes. With

"regular" particulars, particularized natures are too thick. They are bloblike. Much of the particularized nature of a thing, if one can so speak, is irrelevant to a particular case of the thing's resembling something else. But the tropes will have (or rather will be) particularized natures exactly adapted to supporting particular resemblances. They seem excellent substitutes for universal properties.

Well then, it may be said, why should not a natural class view take up the doctrine of particularized nature also? In the trope version, the class of five-kilograms-exact tropes would be a class of the highest unity, but in virtue of the particularized nature of the tropes.

But would not this move pretty much turn the Natural Class theory into the Resemblance theory? Consider a class of tropes having the highest degree of unity, where this unity is supposed to spring from the nature of the tropes involved. Such tropes would exactly resemble each other, and this exact resemblance, also, would flow from the particularized natures. The only way then to differentiate the Natural Class theory from the Resemblance theory would seem to be the following: In the Natural Class theory the particularized natures determine that the class has the highest degree of unity, which in turn determines that all the members resemble exactly. In the Resemblance theory, the particularized natures determine the exact resemblances directly.

Not much difference there. But any difference that there is appears to favor the Resemblance theory, for it *analyzes* the highest degree of unity in terms of something that seems more primitive, namely, resemblance. The property of the whole (its unity) is determined by the resemblances of its parts.

Third, there is a problem about causality (Chapter 2, Section VI). When a thing acts, it acts in virtue of certain of its properties. On a natural class view, possession of a property by a particular will be a matter of that particular's being a member of a certain class. But if we work with ordinary things rather than tropes, what has the remainder of the class to do with the action of the thing? It is simply the thing that acts. This suggests that we want an account of properties which, unlike the natural class view, puts them *in rebus*, in the things that act.

A trope view at least lets us identify the cause somewhat more precisely. The thing acts in virtue of its having a trope of a certain sort (a mass trope, or whatever). But what makes it a trope of a certain sort? On a natural class view, the *class* of tropes of which it is a member still has something to do with making it a trope of a certain sort: the five-kilograms-exact sort, for instance. A trope view that works with exact resemblances does even better. For on this view the relations of exact resemblance that hold between the class of tropes in question spring from the particularized nature of the trope. This particularized nature lies within the thing that acts, so it really is *that trope* that acts.

A Natural Class theory might adopt particularized natures and make the unity of the class of tropes spring from these natures. But we have just seen that this move makes the Natural Class theory almost indistinguishable from the Resemblance view. I think that the arguments reviewed in this section, Wolterstorff's argument, the argument that properties are prior to their classes, and the argument from causality, give us good reason to choose a resemblance version of the Trope theory instead of a natural class account.

## IX. Swapping of Tropes

The difficulty now to be canvassed is probably not a major one. But it is of interest because, if real, it holds for *all* philosophies of tropes, including the resemblance version.

Suppose that *a* has property P but lacks Q, while *b* has property Q but lacks P. In general, at least, it makes sense to say that *a* might have had Q and not P, while *b* might have had P but not Q. For instance, it is possible that two atoms in different excited states might each have had the state that characterizes the other.

Suppose now that we are dealing with property tropes, and that the two tropes involved, P' and P", resemble exactly. Since the two tropes are wholly distinct particulars, it appears to make sense that instead of *a* having P' and *b* having P", the two tropes should have been swapped.

But this is a somewhat unwelcome consequence. The swap lies under suspicion of changing nothing. And now we notice that given a universals analysis, with *a* being P and *b* being P, there is nothing to change. You cannot swap an entity, the universal property P, with itself. One up to universals.

This argument will fail if we take the view advocated by C. B. Martin that properties and relations are nontransferable (see Section II of this chapter). But this restricting of the way that possibilities are preserved under recombination is equally an ontological cost for a trope theorist.

## X. Tropes with Universals

A brief note on the position that admits both tropes and universals, with tropes being typed by their instantiating of universals. We have already seen (Chapter 5, Section I) that this might be an appropriate standpoint for those who think of universals as dwelling in a separate realm from the space-time realm. For then the tropes will break up the blob of a particular, and turn it, more plausibly, into a layer cake.

But if one rejects universals in a separate realm, thus rejecting uninstantiated universals and bringing universals down to earth, presumably as attributes of substances (particulars), then either the universals or the tropes are redundant. Either get rid of universals and, perhaps, embrace a trope version of Resemblance Nominalism or else cut out the middlemen, namely, the tropes.

If we go the second way, as I incline to do, then the theory of states of affairs will serve to explain all *apparent* reference to tropes. 'The illness of the center-forward' or 'the whiteness of the paper' need not be thought of as making reference to tropes of *being ill* or *whiteness*. Rather they can be taken as referring to states of affairs, the foward's being ill, this paper's being white, which involve only (thin) particulars and universals. These states of affairs, although involving universals, will be particular.

# CHAPTER SEVEN

# Summing Up

It is time to bring the matter to a conclusion. Metaphysicians should not expect any certainties in their inquiries. One day, perhaps, the subject will be transformed, but for the present the philosopher can do no more than survey the field as conscientiously as he or she can, taking note of the opinions and arguments of predecessors and contemporaries, and then make a fallible judgment arrived at and backed up as rationally as he or she knows how.

Of all the results that have been argued for here, the most secure, I believe, is the real existence of properties and relations. Whether they be universals or particulars is a more delicate matter, and just what properties and relations are required may be obscure, and in any case not for the philosopher to determine. But I hope that the arguments of Chapters 2 and 3, criticizing the versions of the Natural Class and Resemblance theories that try to do without properties and relations, will be thought weighty. Blobs are out; we require layer cakes. Reality must have more fundamental structure than the stricter Nominalisms allow. The introduction of properties and relations then involves, I argued, the admission of states of affairs (facts) into our ontology.

As between the Natural Class and the Resemblance theory, though condemning both for omitting properties and relations from our "ontological assay," if forced to choose, I take the Resemblance theory. At least it tries to give an analysis of the notion of a natural class, a notion that gives one the feeling that it should be analyzable. The group of arguments of which Wolterstorff's argument from the identity conditions of classes may stand as a representative seems to me to create great difficulties for the Natural Class theory. The Resemblance theory is in any case preferable and is greatly improved, I believe, by the clear recognition that it must introduce *particularized natures* on which, as terms, the relations of resemblance are internally founded.

Passing to the layer-cake theories, those that admit properties and relations, I would put the view that particulars are bundles of universals last. The problems involved with Identity of Indiscernibles and the difficulty of constructing the bundle appear to me to be too formidable.

Brushing aside the uneconomical view that admits both tropes and universals, we have a choice in Trope theory between natural class and resemblance views. The same sort of consideration that favors resemblances rather than natural classes of "regular" particulars seems to me to favor a Trope theory *with resemblance*. And although it is orthodox to bundle the tropes, I doubt if they are really well suited to be the substance of the world. We do better, with Locke and C. B. Martin, to hold the trope view in a substance-attribute form.

Our final two contenders, then, I suggest, are a Universals theory and a Trope Resemblance theory, each held in a substance-attribute form. How do we adjudicate between these two?

The Trope theory in its resemblance and substance-attribute form seems to me to face two unpleasantnesses. The first is relatively minor. It is the possibility of swapping exactly resembling tropes, to which attention was drawn in Section IX of Chapter 6. It is a somewhat implausible 'possibility', and is excluded by the substitution of universals for tropes.

The second difficulty is more serious, I think. It is the fact that the features of resemblance, what we have called the

Axioms of Resemblance, would be explained with the greatest naturalness, simplicity, and economy if resemblance of nature was always identity of nature, either partial or complete identity. The difficulty, it will be remembered, is that the Axioms of Resemblance can be derived from the properties of identity provided that it is allowed that resemblance can be analyzed in terms of identity, that is, in terms of universals (Chapter 5, Section X). A Resemblance theory must treat this as a mere metaphysical coincidence between the properties of resemblance and the properties of identity. It is a serious difficulty for any resemblance analysis that the irreducibility of resemblance is so implausible an irreducibility.

What of the difficulties faced by the Universals theory? It might be thought that a great difficulty lies in its strange primitive: the cross-categorial and fundamental tie or nexus of instantiation. The Resemblance theory has no such problem because its tie of resemblance is an internal relation, supervening upon the particularized natures of the resembling things.

I do not think that instantiation involves any special difficulty for the Universals theory. Barring the postulation of a special nontransferability for tropes, we have seen the need for states of affairs for *all* layer-cake theories, including those involving tropes. If tropes are the attributes of substances, which I have argued is the best view of the matter, then a fundamental tie or nexus is involved, that is, there will be states of affairs involving substances, which are particulars, having properties, and also substances standing in relation to each other. If the bundle conception is correct, then a bundling tie (compresence) is still involved, and relations hold between bundles. Instantiations are just states of affairs involving universals and seem to involve no more paradox or difficulty than states of affairs involving tropes.

Where I do see trouble for a Universals theory is the question of the resemblance of universals. Once universals are admitted, it must also be admitted that universals themselves can be ordered and grouped by resemblance relations. These relations, however, involve less than exact resemblance. (*Two* universals could not resemble exactly!)

The vital question, then, is whether this less than exact resemblance of universals is or is not analyzable. My idea is that it is analyzable, analyzable in terms of a partial, an incomplete, identity of constituents of the universals involved, where these constituents are themselves universals. (In a Trope Resemblance theory, it would be a matter of exact resemblance of some, but only some, constituents of the inexactly resembling tropes.)

If this analysis of the inexact resemblance of universals can be carried through, then the Universals theory is considerably strengthened. But if it cannot be carried through, the theory is weakened, because the inexact resemblances will presumably have to be taken as unanalyzable primitives, strengthening the notion that exact resemblance is no more than the highest degree of this primitive.

So, a great deal turns on whether the analysis of the inexact resemblance of universals can be carried through. I think that it can be carried through, but it faces some formidable ontological and epistemological difficulties. A key question here is the nature of *quantities*. A quantity is for me a family of property universals bound together by inexact but systematic resemblances, but resemblances that involve identical constituents of the universals involved (see Armstrong 1988b). Here is an important area for further work.

Another important question is the nature of laws of nature, a question that I have not had space to address here. I think that they are irreducibly higher-order relations (or necessitation or probabilification) holding between universals (Armstrong 1983). I believe this view has great advantages. It solves the numerous problems that beset a regularity or Humean account of laws. It promises, I think, to point towards a solution of the Problem of Induction. Induction becomes an "abductive" or explanatory inference from observed regularities to a relationship between universals (inference to the best explanation). The hypothesized relationship then permits a deduction of conclusions about unobserved cases where the antecedent universal is instantiated. (See Armstrong 1983, pp. 52–59 and 103–106, and for a similar line of argument about induction, John Foster 1983.) This sort of account of induction would not be available to a Trope theory.

At the same time, though, the theory is controversial. Sophisticated Humeans, such as David Lewis (see, for instance, pp. xii and xvii of Lewis 1986d), think that such a relation between universals is a mystery whose link to the unobserved cases is magic.

Therefore, the fate of the Universals theory may turn on the questions of the inexact resemblance of universals and of the nature of laws. But if both questions go as I surmise that they will go, the Universals theory seems ahead of even the best Trope theory.

Drawing a figure from the game of chess, Mark Johnston has suggested to me that the dispute between a suitably sophisticated theory of universals and a suitably sophisticated theory of tropes can only be decided in the end game. Maybe. We are probably only at the beginning of the middle game as yet.

We have seen in Chapter 6 the remarkable way that the Universals and Trope theories, when thought through, turn out to run parallel in many respects. We may in the end have to reconsider an idea of H. H. Price's (1953, Ch. 1, pp. 30–32) that Universals and Resemblance theories are no more than "alternative languages," although, unlike Price, we will surely need to move to a trope version of a Resemblance theory.

At any rate, the Problem of Universals is alive and well and may commend itself to those happy few who feel the intellectual fascination in what D. C. Williams called "grubbing around in the roots of being."

# REFERENCES

Abbott, F. E. (1886) *Scientific Theism*, Macmillan.

Adams, R. (1979) Primitive Thisness and Primitive Identity, *Journal of Philosophy* 76.

Aristotle. *Basic Works*, ed. R. McKeon, Random House, 1941.

Armstrong, D. M. (1978a) *Nominalism and Realism*, vol. 1 of *Universals and Scientific Realism*, Cambridge University Press.

———. (1978b) *A Theory of Universals*, vol. 2 of *Universals and Scientific Realism*, Cambridge University Press.

———. (1980) Against "Ostrich Nominalism": A Reply to Michael Devitt, *Pacific Philosophical Quarterly* 61.

———. (1983) *What Is a Law of Nature?* Cambridge University Press.

———. (1988a) Can a Naturalist Believe in Universals? in *Science in Reflection*, ed. E. Ullmann-Margalit, Kluwer Academic Publishers.

———. (1988b) Are Quantities Relations? *Philosophical Studies* 54.

———. (1989) *A Combinatorial Theory of Possibility*, Cambridge University Press.

Bar-Elli, G. (1988) Can a Naturalist Believe in Universals? A Comment, in *Science in Reflection*, ed. E. Ullmann-Margalit, Kluwer Academic Publishers.

Bergmann, G. (1967) *Realism*, University of Wisconsin Press.

Blanshard, B. (1939) *The Nature of Thought*, Allen and Unwin.

———. (1962) *Reason and Analysis*, Open Court.

Butler, J. *The Analogy of Religion*, Everyman, 1906.

Campbell, K. K. (1981) The Metaphysic of Abstract Particulars, *Midwest Studies in Philosophy*, vol. 6, ed. P. A. French, T. E. Uehling, and H. K. Wettstein, University of Minnesota Press.

———. (forthcoming) *Abstract Particulars*, Blackwell.

Denkel, A. (1989) Real Resemblances, *Philosophical Quarterly* 39.

Devitt, M. (1980) "Ostrich Nominalism" or "Mirage Realism"? *Pacific Philosophical Quarterly* 61.

141

REFERENCES

Foster, J. (1983) Induction, Explanation and Natural Necessity, *Proceedings of the Aristotelian Society*, vol. 83.

Goodman, N. (1966) *The Structure of Appearance*, 2nd ed., Bobbs-Merrill.

Hume, D. *A Treatise of Human Nature*, 2 vols., Everyman, 1911.

Jackson, F. (1977) Statements about Universals, *Mind* 76.

Küng, G. (1967) *Ontology and the Logistic Analysis of Language*, rev. ed., Reidel.

Leibniz, G. W. *The Leibniz-Clarke Correspondence*, ed. H. G. Alexander, Manchester University Press, 1956.

Lewis, D. (1983) New Work for a Theory of Universals, *Australasian Journal of Philosophy* 61.

————. (1986a) *On the Plurality of Worlds*, Blackwell.

————. (1986b) Against Structural Universals, *Australasian Journal of Philosophy* 64.

————. (1986c) Comment on Forrest and Armstrong, *Australasian Journal of Philosophy* 64.

————. (1986d) *Philosophical Papers*, vol. 2, Oxford University Press.

Martin, C. B. (1980) Substance Substantiated, *Australasian Journal of Philosophy* 58.

Matthews, G. B., and S. M. Cohen (1968) The One and the Many, *Review of Metaphysics* 21.

McTaggart, J. McT. E. (1921) *The Nature of Existence*, 2 vols., Cambridge University Press.

Pap, A. (1959) Nominalism, Empiricism and Universals: 1, *Philosophical Quarterly* 9.

Plato. Philebus, trans. A. E. Taylor, in *Plato: Philebus and Epinomis*, ed. R. Klibansky, Nelson, 1956.

————. *Republic*, trans. F. Cornford, Oxford University Press, 1941.

Price, H. H. (1953) *Thinking and Experience*, Hutchinson.

Quilter, J. (1985) What Has Properties? *Proceedings of the Russellian Society*, Philosophy Dept., Sydney University, 10.

Quine, W. V. (1961) 'On What There Is,' in *From a Logical Point of View*, by W. V. Quine, Harper & Row.

————. (1980) Soft Impeachment Disowned, *Pacific Philosophical Quarterly* 61.

Quinton, A. (1957) Properties and Classes, *Proceedings of the Aristotelian Society*, vol. 58.

————. (1973) *The Nature of Things*, Routledge and Kegan Paul.

Russell, B. (1912) *The Problems of Philosophy*, Home University Library.

———. (1940) *An Inquiry into Meaning and Truth*, Allen and Unwin.

———. (1948) *Human Knowledge, Its Scope and Limits*, Allen and Unwin.

———. (1959) *My Philosophical Development*, Allen and Unwin.

Seargent, D. A. J. (1985) *Plurality and Continuity, an Essay in G. F. Stout's Theory of Universals*, Martinus Nijhoff.

Sellars, W. (1963) Philosophy and the Scientific Image of Man, in *Science, Perception and Reality*, by W. F. Sellars, Routledge and Kegan Paul.

Skyrms, B. (1981) Tractarian Nominalism, *Philosophical Studies* 40.

Sober, Elliott. (1982) Why Logically Equivalent Predicates May Pick Out Different Properties, *American Philosophical Quarterly* 19.

Stout, G. F. (1921) *The Nature of Universals and Propositions*, Oxford University Press (British Academy Lecture), reprinted in G. F. Stout, *Studies in Philosophy and Psychology*, Macmillan, 1930.

———. (1936) Universals Again, *Proceedings of the Aristotelian Society*, supp. vol. 15.

Tooley, M. (1987) *Causation*, Clarendon Press.

Williams, D. C. (1966) "The Elements of Being," in *The Principles of Empirical Realism*, by D. C. Williams, Charles Thomas.

Wittgenstein, L. (1953) *Philosophical Investigations*, Blackwell.

———. (1961) *Tractatus Logico-Philosophicus*, trans. D. F. Pears and B. F. McGuinness, Routledge and Kegan Paul.

Wolterstorff, N. (1970) *On Universals*, University of Chicago Press.